Hardened Images:

The Western Media and the Marginalization of Africa

Asgede Hagos

Africa World Press, Inc.

P.O. Box 1892
Trenton, NJ 08607

P.O. Box 48
Asmara, ERITREA

Africa World Press, Inc.

P.O. Box 1892
Trenton, NJ 08607

P.O. Box 48
Asmara, ERITREA

Book Design: Krystal Jackson

Library of Congress Cataloging-in-Publication Data

Hagos, Asgede.
  Hardened images : the Western media and the marginalization of Africa / Asgede Hagos.
      p. cm.
Includes bibliographical references (p.   ) and index.
    ISBN 0-86543-900-1 -- ISBN   0-86543-901-X (pbk.)
  1.   Africa--Foreign relations--United States. 2. United States--Foreign relations--Africa. 3.   Africa--Foreign relations--1960-
4.   United States--Foreign relations--1977-1981. 5.   United States--Foreign relations--1981-1989. 6.   Press and politics--United States--History--20th century. 7.   National liberation movements--Africa--Foreign public opinion, American. 8.   Public opinion--United States--History--20th century.   I. Title.
    DT38.7 .H34   2000
    327.7306--dc21   00-010135

To the memory of my father, Hagos Kidane;
my mother, Tabotu Andebrhan; and my brothers
Araya, Yohannes, Seyoum and Gebar;
also to the Eritrean men and women,
including my older brother Gebar,
my nephews Habtu, Michael, Menghis,
Yeman, and my niece Abrehet, who sacrificed
their lives so that their people can be free;
also Kidane, Andu and Goitom who died so young.

CONTENTS

TABLES

FIGURES

Those who hold the power also tell the stories.

—Plato

Acknowledgments

There are many people who made this book possible and, because it is impossible to list all of them, I would like to express my thanks and gratitude to at least some of them.

I owe much to my parents, my brothers and sisters for the spirit of fortitude they instilled in me which kept me going even when at times the going looked bleak and difficult.

My special thanks and gratitude also go out to my family without whose love and continuous encouragement this research would not have been completed. A special thanks to my wife, Aster Bocrai, for her support, encouragement and the sacrifice she had to make to see me through this project. And to my children—my daughter, Lula, and my son, Michael (Hilal)—for being a continuous source of inspiration and for the love that could come only from them which made the road I had to travel a little brighter and the load a little lighter.

My profound and eternal debt of gratitude goes to Drs. Mbye B. Cham, Sulayman S. Nyang, and Abas Malek for their valuable insight, suggestions and candid advice when I initially undertook this task. My particular appreciation extends to all my friends and colleagues for their confidence and moral support throughout this process.

INTRODUCTION

This book is the product of a lifetime of formal and informal investigation into the attitudes and behaviors of the Western press toward Africa, its peoples, and especially its struggles for freedom and dignity. It started with many of the questions, puzzled thoughts and doubts that these channels of communication left me with early in my career as a journalist in Africa. These various forms of expressions of concern about Western media coverage of the continent also persisted through the next phase of my life as a journalist and a mass communications educator in the United States.

The nagging questions were also prompted by my growing recognition of the power of the international press to shape world public opinion to a degree never seen before and Africa's increasing dependency on it to tell the African story as well as define its experience. The implications are frightening when a people have to rely on foreign organizations for news and information about their own countries. Yet, that is the case in many African countries today. I also realized early in my life that the press and the rest of the mass media, including Hollywood, don't work in a vacuum. The way it covers Africa and its struggles for freedom depends not only on the attitudes and behaviors of the international media gatekeepers, but also on those of Western governments, with serious implications for Africa's place, visibility and acceptability in the international political and economic system.

Then when the formal investigation started in graduate school, the nagging queries, puzzles, and doubts merged into one central research question: How does the interplay between the press and the government in the United States, the center of the international political and economy system, affect Africa's visibility and acceptability in the world, and its struggles for freedom? Or, looking at it from another dimension, does the international press contribute to the growing marginalization of the continent?

The central purpose of this study is therefore to explore and describe the nature of this interplay between the United States press and the American state in the foreign policy making arena, with a special focus on Africa. It takes a close look at the role of today's powerful press in society and examines how the interplay helps shape the foreign policy debate in the United States. The examination focuses on the interaction between the elite press and foreign policy makers on a key African issue, the national liberation movement, considered to be on the cutting edge of change in the continent because it represents the last and often violent stage in the process of decolonization. The study is centered on three case studies—the national liberation movements of South Africa, Eritrea and Western Sahara, which seem to represent the last and probably the most complex and difficult stage in the decolonization of Africa. United States policy toward all three movements, though it varied from territory to territory, had a great deal to do with the complexity and difficulty surrounding this phase and may even have prolonged the completion of the decolonization process in the continent. It attempts to see if the press challenges the basic assumptions and practices of United States policy for Africa in general, and as the policy relates to the three-armed struggles for freedom in particular.

Using content analysis as the principal methodological tool of inquiry, I have analyzed editorials from two elite newspapers, the *New York Times* and the *Washington Post,* as well as documents from the official organ of United

States foreign policy, the *United States Department of State Bulletin*, covering an eight-year period (January 1977-December 1984). The study period spans over two consecutive United States administrations—one Democratic, one Republican; one liberal, the other conservative.

Although much has been written with a focus on the nexus between these two institutions as it relates to domestic issues, very little has been undertaken examining their interaction in the foreign policy and foreign policy making arena. The literature indicates that, though the press may disagree with the policy makers on policy tactics and style, generally speaking, it does not seem to challenge the basic approach of United States foreign policy on Africa. Both institutions of the press and the state seem unwilling to see and accept as noble and just the internal factors that lead to armed struggle for basic freedom and human dignity in Africa, as opposed to other regions, especially Europe. The literature review also showed that both institutions tend to view such struggles as products of external factors.

The relationship between these two institutions on domestic issues is characterized by what seems like a love-hate or cooperation-competition relationship depending on their sometimes diverging, some other times converging interests. Sometimes the press is viewed as the watchdog whose primary function is to ensure that the state does not overstep the bounds set for a legitimate institution of governance. However, there are times when it acts like a lapdog whose main mission is to protect, legitimize and reinforce the status quo. For example, the nature of that relationship tends to change when the two institutions are focusing on foreign policy matters, where the press, like the state, is mainly guided by American national interest, and not the lofty ideals of journalism, though it might profess otherwise. The state, which is entrusted with the responsibility of foreign policy matters, generally leads the dance in this arena—generally, but not always, as we will see in some of the cases in this book.

This interplay of support and cooperation is very much evident when the two institutions converge on issues relating to Africa. However, the data also shows the other dimension of this institutional dance—a dimension, not of support and harmony, but of competition and influence.

There is no question the press, despite its portrayal of its own role as a neutral link and disinterested medium of information, is an active participant or at least very influential in the foreign policy making arena. During the period of this study, its presence and influence in U.S. policy making process for Africa was very visible.

Each of the following six chapters will examine the different dimensions of that relationship. Chapter 1, in addition to raising the key questions and issues that undergird the discussion, lays down the theoretical framework that guided the study and helped sort out what the press says it does and what it actually does—and why. The questions and issues raised focus on the distorted and hardened images of Africa, its people, and its struggles for freedom in the Western mass media and how that actually contributes to the marginalization of the continent. The chapter looks into the legacy of neglect of Africa, the most central of the major regions of the world. Though it is clear the United States press does not function independent of all other institutional actors in the society, the chapter puts the spotlight on it in order to examine its role in the hardening of the negative images that have characterized Africa's portrayals in the West over the last centuries.

The organization of the rest of the chapters is as follows: Chapter 2, which provides the background to the issues explored in the previous chapter provides the case studies on which the investigation is based. In an attempt to put the issues within an historical context, Chapter 2 looks back into United States foreign policy for Africa during the post-World War II years, but especially in relation to three key African struggles for freedom from 1977 to 1984, during the Carter and Reagan years. The selected case studies were three national liberation struggles that raged during this period in three African territories, Eritrea, Western Sahara and South Africa.

The data, which comes mostly from the editorials of the two selected daily elite newspapers and the *United States Department of State Bulletin,* the official United States foreign policy organ, is presented in Chapters 3 and 4. Chapter 3 covers the official documents over the eight years of the period of this study pertaining to the three movements, while Chapter 4 focuses on the editorials from the *Washington Post* and the *New York Times.* The main findings of this study are also discussed in this chapter, and analyzed and interpreted in Chapter 4. The interpretation was necessary because the data included editorial and policy information that was sometimes clouded in diplomatic and ideological messages. Chapter 5 examines the two dimensions of the interplay, one of influence and the other of support. On one level of the relationship, we see the institutions trying to influence each other's agenda; the other dimension shows interplay of support, with each institution reinforcing the other's position on the key issues. For example, the chapter looks into how the press reinforces the state's distorted attitude toward African national liberation movements and how that reveals itself in the editorials of the two elite dailies. Chapter 6 then ties together the different strands of the questions and issues discussed throughout the book to provide a summation as well as conclusions of the study.

Chapter 1

A LEGACY OF NEGLECT

As we enter the new millennium, Africa continues to be ravaged by conflicts—some old and some new—stretching from Sierra Leone to Somalia, from the Sudan to Rwanda, and from the Great Lakes Region to the Horn of Africa. In fact, the biggest conflict in the world in 1998 and 1999 was in Africa, a conflict that many saw as the completion of one that was thought to have ended in 1991 with the liberation of Eritrea after 30 years of a brutal armed struggle. Judging by its impact on human lives, the new conflict between Eritrea and Ethiopia, which erupted in May 1998 in the form of a border skirmish, has certainly been the most murderous in the world today. It has claimed tens of thousands of Ethiopian and Eritrean lives, and has resulted in the displacement of hundreds of thousands on both sides of the border.

Judging by any journalistic standards, this and many of the other conflicts in the continent, the most central and second largest of the major regions, warrant a great deal of international press attention. Yet, on the attention radar of the Western press, especially that of the United States, which dominates the international mass media, these conflicts don't even represent a blip. What is even more disheartening is that we see little change in the way the Western press has been covering Africa and Africans the last half century, the post-independence period. Sometimes one even finds eerie similarities between today's Western press attitude toward the continent and at the turn of the last millennium, except that the expression of that attitude one hundred years later is a little more subtle.

Many see this legacy of neglect of Africa and Africans as the result of the interplay between the institutions of the press and the state in the West. When President Bill Clinton went to Africa on an extended visit in the spring of 1998, the first time a sitting United States president to do so, many people, especially Africans and African Americans, hoped against hope that Africa would receive its fair share of attention from United States foreign policy makers, and that African Americans have finally found a voice in the foreign policy making arena. That hope was based on the assumption that the United States government influences United States press attention of a region. This book explores that assumption and examines the nature of the interplay between the institutions of the state and the press. However, the attention level that was expected didn't come to pass, partly due to the United States government's failure to sustain the interest it showed in the spring of 1998, and partly due to a long legacy of neglect of Africa and Africans by the American press. Such neglect has been taken as the norm when it comes to press coverage of the continent.

The implications of this kind of attitude towards the continent are grave. The extent and nature of the problem, as well as some of the answers to the question why Africa is the world's most ignored major region by the Western press, are now coming for the first time from inside the newsrooms, a reflection of the presence of a few African American voices in some capacity as gatekeepers serving United States news organizations. Trevor Coleman of the *Detroit Free Press* talks of a fellow journalist who told him of "a *Washington Post* editor commenting years ago that the West ought to build a fence around Africa, peek over it now and then, and after 100 years, tear it down to see what's left." He said the story "certainly speaks to the prevailing attitude of major United States media when it comes to Africa. It is essentially that of a continent, besieged by an unrelenting series of horrific tragedies, hopelessly backward, above and beyond redemption." The *Free Press* editorial writer challenges his fellow members of the National Conference of Editorial Writers to "seek to demystify Africa" (1997, 25).

In yet another rare, but growing internal challenge to the way the American mass media have been covering Africa, a group of minority reporters and editors of *The Los Angeles Times* a few years ago criticized its paper's depiction of "the world as Africa-less." In in-house electronic messages, the group, known as the Unitary Caucus, charged that in the paper's world survey, Europe was "given two separate categories while Africa, one of the largest and most populous continent on the planet, is dealt with two sentences under 'Other.'" Furthermore, the coalition of minority journalists charged that the little coverage that makes it into the pages of their newspaper was characterized by distortion of the African reality. It portrays the region, the group said, through the prism of Eurocentrism. The group also criticized a *Times'* story which lamented "the long, sad decline of Africa" and described the deterioration of the Angolan capital of Luanda from "a pristine, bayside city of Portuguese architecture." In internal electronic messages, the members of the Caucus rightly asked, "Long, sad decline from what? From colonialism? Is the *Times* yearning for the 'pristine' days of white rule?" Another memo charged that an article, which said Ghanaian President Jerry Rawling's "reputation for personal probity sets him apart from the rest of the continent's leaders," ended up "besmirching the entire continent" (Kurtz 1993, E1).

Challenge to this kind of coverage of the continent and its people are not new. However, this conflict between a member of America's elite press, which sets the news agenda for the rest of the United States press, and a small group of American reporters and editors of African descent provides a rare glimpse from inside of America's mainstream newsrooms into how the Western press covers the African reality. The incident provides some insight into the factors that may contribute to African marginalization to which many African and other communication scholars have been drawing attention for many decades. More specifically, it brought out the two basic problems—some would say two sides of the same problem—that characterize Western press coverage of Africa: a combination of neglect and distortion, or omission and commission, if you will, both of which contribute to the marginalization of the continent. As Mencher says, "A publication or [TV or radio] station can be assessed by its wastebasket as by its columns and newscasts, for the sins of omission are as serious as those of commission" (1997, 67).

However, the depth and breath of this double-edged approach to African coverage can be seen even clearer in the way the Western mass media have been covering Africa's armed and protracted struggles for freedom and basic dignity, represented in the national liberation movement—the highest and last stage in the process of decolonization of the continent. One can see this in the near-total neglect of these struggles, as we will see later in the struggles in South Africa, Eritrea and Western Sahara. One can also see this in the characterization of these struggles in the very little media attention the movements receive; they have been portrayed, not as the noble human endeavors as in Eastern or Western Europe, but as the embodiments of evil, anti-Western, and anti-Christian—all the characteristics of any issue that is bound to be relegated to the margins of the Western-dominated international system.

The memos of the *Los Angeles Times* reporters and editors also revealed some of what many scholars pointed out as the other deadly sins that the Western mass media commit in their coverage of Africa: the tendency to look at the entire continent as one undifferentiated mass, and the constant attempt to portray the region through the prism of Eurocentrism. It also points up the need for more diverse voices in America's newsrooms to bring sensitivity to, if not increase in African coverage in the international mass media.

The coverage, based on an information selection process guided mainly by ideology, but also race in this case, has had serious implications for Africa's visibility and acceptability in the world. Today, there is no question that of the major regions of the world, Africa is the most invisible continent, shoved to the margins of the world's political and economic systems, and into the furthest recesses of international consciousness. Confined to the periphery of the system, more than four decades since Ghana's independence in 1957 ushered in the era of independence, the continent is still viewed by the West and, as a result, portrayed by its media outlets, not as an independent actor in international relations, but as an inconsequential extension of the former colonial powers in all phases of that relationship. In the words of a French diplomat, "Economically speaking, if all of black Africa, with the exception of South Africa, were to disappear in a flood, the global cataclysm would be approximately nonexistent" (Bering-Jensen 1992, 9). Even in their own countries, Africans are not viewed as primary players, "precluded from defining events that affect them and from positioning Africa on its own terms within the world community" (Fair 1992, 117).

The developing regions of the world are seriously disadvantaged by the prevailing pattern of information flow— a one-way flow from the Northern Hemisphere, the homes of the industrialized nations, with the developing regions at the receiving end. Africa has been the most disadvantaged of all. The basic relationship between Africa and the West, which is characterized by dependency, exploitation, and domination of the former by the latter, was bound to lead to the present state of invisibility or peripheralization. Here, peripheralization implies at least two important things: unequal relationship and a certain degree of powerlessness in relation to the center of the system. Explaining the first characteristic of this phenomena, Adedeji says: "At first level, sets of unequal or antagonistic relationships come to mind that exercise power even when they are perceived rather than actual: fast-track/slow track (or on-track/off track), center/periphery, majority/minority, possession/dispossession, independence/dependence, superiority/inferiority, and dominance/subordination all are necessary and sometimes sufficient conditions to marginality to arise" (1993, 1). On the margins are the regions and nations that are at the receiving end of the system, while at the center are the powerful, rich, former colonial nations, which have been defining the terms of the relationships. The nature of the relationship or degree of peripheralization can constantly change depending on how important the subject or nation in-question is perceived to be to and by the center.

As the relationship between the Center and the Periphery, the rural and urban sectors, in any country is based on exploitation of the latter by the former, the structural relationship between the developing and the developed nations can be viewed from the same structural schema (Kruijer 1987). This structural approach to the study of international relations came in response to the dominant paradigm of development (Frank 1969, Beltran 1974 and 1976, Galtung 1977). During the last three decades, scholars have shown how regions like Africa, the most central of them all, have been pushed to the margins, with the West acting as the Center of the global system, and how this unbalanced structural relationship encouraged the exploitation of the Periphery. The Western press, as an integral part of the Center, plays a critical role in the latter's relationship with the Periphery and as the voice of the dominant forces in the Center by creating a single consensus among all sectors of the social order based on the ideology of the dominant forces.

However, why is this most central of the continents pushed to the margins, and how, if any, did the Western press contribute to the peripheralization of the region? This work is about one aspect of this complex marginalization process: to explore the role of the Western mass media in the peripheralization of the continent and its struggles for freedom. Though the Western mass media don't operate in a vacuum at both the national and international levels, I have chosen to put the focus on these information channels because there is little research done to examine their role in the peripheralization of the continent. Furthermore, the mass media represent a powerful force on their own. There is a growing awareness of the role of the mass media in influencing the policymaking process, as well as domestic and international public opinion. In fact, Molana says, "In a broad sense, the study of the international flow of information is another approach to the study of international relations—beyond the narrow scope of the mass media and the growing number of technological channels" (1986, vii). The volume of information flowing from the West to the developing countries is increasing. Governments and national leaders are becoming more and more aware of the power of these mostly high-technology-based channels. They have the power to frame, define and shape reality, mostly through a selection process based primarily on ideological orientation. Studies during the last quarter century have shown that these channels of information have the power to frame the issues that define the Third World, its people and the peoples' struggles today.

In this book, we shall look into the role of the press within the context of its relationship with the state. Some of the key questions used to explore the issue deal with the nature of the interplay between the press and the state in setting the public agenda, and whether or not there are any differences in the interaction between the two institutions on domestic issues as opposed to foreign affairs. I have explored these questions in relation to Africa's armed struggles for freedom, representing the last and often violent stage in the process of decolonization of Africa. I have examined the nature of this interplay within the American context in the foreign policymaking arena by analyzing their respective positions on this African issue. In undertaking this analysis, my intention has been to provide a closer look into the attitudes of both the policy makers and the journalists toward armed struggle as a primary means of achieving liberation in three selected territories: South Africa, Eritrea and Western Sahara. Furthermore, I have looked to see if this interaction between these two key institutions limits the diversity of voices in the foreign policy-making process. The main purpose of such an examination has been to see if these two institutions influence each other on key policy issues, and in setting the public policy agenda.

The scope of this study covers two consecutive United States administrations (January 1977 to December 1984), one Democratic, the other Republican, and investigates their respective positions on the three selected African movements vis-à-vis those two elite newspapers, *The New York Times* and *The Washington Post*. Using content analysis as the chief means of inquiry, I have focused on the editorials of these newspapers pertaining to the continent in general and the three selected territories in particular to test if they question the goals of United States policy in Africa and to examine their attitudes toward the liberation movements.

As a result, this book takes a critical look at the interaction between these key institutions to examine if it has any impact on United States relations with Africa and the portrayal of Africa's struggles for freedom. A more specific goal of this work is to describe and try to measure the effect of such an interaction on an African issue—the national liberation movement—considered on the cutting edge of change in the continent. The national liberation movement is the highest stage in the anti-colonial struggle in the continent. Part of the explanation why Africa is left on the periphery of the periphery of the global system may be in the relationship between these two institutions in the developed countries, especially the United States, whose mass media set the tone for the rest of the Western mass media.

A Framework of Analysis

Any serious examination to determine the factors and forces that may have contributed to the marginalization of Africa should include a critical analysis of the modern channels of communication, which have the power to reach out to billions of people instantly and directly across the world, thereby influencing and reinforcing international attitudes and behavior. Such an examination should begin with a serious look at the press's relationships with the key institutions of the society, especially the state, the principal institutional actor in international relations. However, there are differing perspectives on the nature and extent of this interaction between these institutions.

Under the classical democratic theory, the press is supposed to play roles ranging from serving as a watchdog to see the state does not go beyond the constitutional limits set for it, to being a bridge linking up the government and the governed. However, as we will see below, there is a lack of consensus on the intended role of the institution in society, its actual practice and the way it portrays itself continue to generate debate on the normative and working theories of the mass media. This is partly due to the way the press itself portrays its role in a democracy. Studies examining the mass media's professed role, as well as their growing reach—now expanding at an overwhelming speed as we approach the third millennium—have not been able to provide structural explanations to what looked like contradictions between the normative and working theories of the press, or, when, for example, the press is working in its self-interest, while at the same time trying to protect other societal institutions, especially in times of crisis. Furthermore, some of the structural bias that is becoming more and more evident in news coverage seems to help perpetuate a one-dimensional view of the Africa and Africans.

The second relevant perspective, through which we will examine the interplay between the state and the press, is the critical cultural theory, which looks at the press as an adjunct of the state.

* * *

Though the primary purpose of this book is to examine if and how the interplay between the United States press and American foreign policy makers affects Africa's foreign media coverage and if and how that may have contributed to the marginalization of the continent and its struggles for freedom, it is important to start with the media's role in a democracy to set the ideal standards against which the actual performance of the press will be examined and compared. The degree of conceptual and practical confusion about the role of the mass media in a democracy has been pointed out by many media scholars and practitioners and is evident in the findings of many studies. This has implications for United States media coverage of the rest of the world because correspondents, scholars and media consumers constantly confuse normative and working theories of the mass media.

Under the classical democratic theory, the press is viewed as a facilitator for the state. One of the enduring principles that speak to the special role the press plays in a society is that "a popular government, without popular information, or the means of acquiring it, is but a prologue to a farce or a tragedy; or perhaps both" (Madison: 1865, 276).

The press views its role as a neutral link between the government and the governed, a positive catalyst that greases and moves the wheels of democracy. This model, whose roots can be traced back to the American and French revolutions of the last quarter of the eighteenth century, assumes that the citizenry has the ultimate power to determine the public policy agenda and the outcomes of such an agenda. It also assumes that a politically vigilant and active populace if sufficiently informed can debate and form wise judgment on the issues. The political vigilance that the people are required to maintain to ensure their sovereignty and rule depends on how well informed the voters are on the issues of the day. This information is supplied primarily by the press and then translated into decisions at the voting booths. Thus, the centrality of a free press or the indispensability of a free flow of information in such a system leaves no room for doubt.

However, the press cannot perform its task as facilitator without a constitutional protection from the whims and coercive powers of the state—hence another face of this complex relationship between the two institutions. At one level, they work together to maintain the status quo and the social system in which they function. At another level, they become adversaries when their interests clash. For example, the press survives and thrives on free flow of information while such a free flow may threaten the existence of the state. Bagdikian argues that to the government a controlled or less flow of information "has come to mean more national security" (1989, 204). The press's watchdog function, which it performs relatively well at the domestic level, is based on this clash of interests between the two. The role of the American press in exposing the scandal of Watergate and the disclosures in the Pentagon Papers are good examples that show how the press in general is vigilant and sometimes aggressive in its domestic coverage of the affairs of the state. Undergirding this aggressive coverage of domestic issues is competition for the shrinking advertising dollar. The intense competition between the press organizations, their publications and other news outlets plays as much a role as journalistic ideals in the coverage of national and local operations. A newspaper is first and foremost a business and those who own and run these organizations use every legal means possible to make a profit and avoid failure.

However, the classical model cannot adequately explain the role of today's modern press, which has its own commercial, institutional and professional interests to protect. For example, the American press, during the last quarter of the 18th century, when it began to experiment with twice-weeklies and thrice-weeklies before the first dailies appeared (with circulation under 5,000), made very little political impact. However, one hundred years later, the newspaper business became big business. What were virtually small, one-man operations grew into complex business institutions valued at millions of dollars.

Among other things, the classical model does not consider the economic imperatives of the press. In fact, Altschull believes that "the press has operated less in terms of what the reading public wanted of it than in terms of what the merchants who supplied the advertising revenue desired" (1984, 63). This is not to imply that the public interest imperative does not have a role or is totally ignored. But, it would be misleading to portray the press of today solely as the disinterested instrument of information it was intended to be under the classical doctrine. The following excerpt from the 1923 American Society of Newspaper Editors' Cannons of Journalism show why this one-sided image persists: "The right of a newspaper to attract and hold readers is restricted by nothing but considerations of public welfare.... Freedom from all obligations except that of fidelity to the public interest is vital.... Freedom of the press is to be guarded as a vital right of mankind" (See Breed 1952, 14-18).

Orren (1987) argues that the classical concept went through many transformations. It was replaced by a party/elite model, in which political parties and the establishment elite played a key role in determining issues and the shapes of their outcomes. However, this too gave way to yet another model of democracy, which Orren calls "media democracy," summing up the current expanded role of the press severely limiting the traditional functions and influence of the political parties. In fact, Orren says, "The media have assumed a greater role in setting the policy agenda, once the exclusive terrain of parties and political leaders" (1987, 10). He further stressed "within a span of a single generation, the American press has been transformed from a nearly invisible spectator to a principal actor in the American political arena, one frequently described as the 'fourth branch' of the American government. We have become a society fueled by information, fast approaching what has been dubbed the 'first amendment regime'" (Orren 1987, 2).

However, this conclusion totally ignores the role of the other institutions, especially that of the state with all its elastic and coercive powers, in setting the public policy agenda. True, because of its growing influence in the society, which is directly proportional to its size and economic clout, the role of the press has greatly expanded and continues to expand. However, it does not have the exclusive and dominant role some have assigned to it.

The problem with these two views is that the models assign either too little or too much role to today's press. The first model, which assumes the supremacy of the people on public issues and in which the press is portrayed as a neutral link, an enterprising watch-dog and a disinterested informational bridge between the other institutions, fails to consider the tremendous transformations that have taken place within the press since the first daily newspapers were born in the 1780s, increasing its presence and impact as a social and political force. The media-democracy model, on the other hand, pushes this development too far and assigns the institution of the press virtual supremacy over the other institutions. That this notion is far from the truth can be seen when one considers the role of the press in time of crisis, like a war, when the state decides on the degree of the flow of information to the public through a system of censorship that has been developed and refined since the American Civil War. But, there is a strong element of truth in Orren's conclusion that recognizes the growing role of the media in the political field. Today, it is practically impossible to understand the process of decision making in the political arena without factoring in the role of the press.

But, how do the institutions of the press and the state interact in the United States? Studies (Cohen 1963, Sigal 1973) indicate that policy makers and reporters view each other as "adversaries." But, are they really? Is there a conflict between how they feel toward each other and what they do in reality? Several works have tried to grapple with these and similar questions. The tremendous growth of both the mass communications industry and the government over the last century, and especially the last four decades, has greatly stimulated interest in many of the social science fields on the interplay of the two institutions. For example, in the last three decades alone, more than 150 studies have investigated the agenda-setting power of the press (Lowery and DeFleur 1983).

Part of the problem has to do with the way the press portrays its interaction with the government. But, the fact is this perceived role of these modern channels of communication does not quite fit their actual practice in today's information society. The practice of the United States media in covering international news is good example. There is a big gap between the portrayed image and the actual practice of today's press. As Arno puts it, in addition to the economic, technological as well as other determinants, the press "must operate within contexts of shared cultural meaning just as other social actors do" (1984, 1). For exam-

14

ple, a shared interest in maintaining the status quo is a characteristic of the institutions of the press and the state. One area where this becomes even clearer, where the press acts more like a friendly lapdog, rather than a watchdog, is in foreign news coverage.

Another perspective that can best explain this complex nature of interplay between the two institutions is that of critical cultural theory. When seen through the prism of critical cultural theory, the role of the press in society and its relationship with other societal institutions becomes clearer. Why one minute the press is viewed as a credible watchdog exposing excesses of the state, and the next minute it acts as a lapdog satisfied with news crumbs thrown its way by the state as in its coverage of the Gulf War, shows the complexity of the relationship between the two institutions. Through the eyes of critical cultural theorists, there is no contradiction between the normative and working theories of the press. Its primary institutional goal is the maintenance of the social order in which the institution of the state plays the most central role. It accomplishes this goal by legitimatizing the status quo when its internal and external legitimacy is called into question and serving as an instrument of social control when that becomes necessary.

The basic assumptions of the new perspective are "centrally concerned with the larger social order and elite's media use and explores the consequences of media use for maintaining elite power" (Baran et al. 1995, 282). The press represents a crucial link in a network of domestic and international institutions whose values are embodied in the ideology on which these communication channels base their coverage. One of these is the institution of the state whose security is of paramount importance to the mass media. As we saw in the 1990 Gulf War, they have also become indispensable actors in international relations, hitherto an exclusive domain of the state.

Switzer said the mass media exist "as an institution mutually reinforcing other institutions in a social formation which can be said to be 'structured in dominance.' Like other institutions, the press embodies economic, political and ideological forms...but it manifests itself primarily as an instrument of ideology in the social formation," (1985, 6). However, when it comes to shaping ideas and influencing public opinion, not all social institutions have the same influence on society. The media are regarded among the most influential in this regard for several reasons, the best being the fact that they put out a great deal of information which is accessible to the public and is regularly disseminated.

In this social formation, the institutions reinforce each other and together they work to strengthen the social system they represent and thrive in. But, there are times when they have to protect individual institutional interests. As a result, while reinforcing each other's existence and interest, they try to influence each other's agenda to fit or benefit their special interests. However, whenever there is a threat either to the system or to any of them, their survival or common interests become of paramount interest. For example, as stated above, in times of war—a potential danger to the institution of the state—the mass media normally abandons their watchdog function in their relationship with the state. Whenever their common interests are served, they combine their forces. Because they are guided by a common ideological orientation, they intuitively work in concert when their common interest required such a strategy.

Stuart Hall identifies the press and the popular culture it produces and distributes as critical cultural tools of the dominant forces of the society. As the key producers and processors of culture, the mass media, an important part of the 'cultural industry' played a critical role in building an ideological consensus (Hall 1985). In explaining how this works, Miliband said the mass media are effective in building "a climate of conformity, not by total suppression of dissent, but by the presentation of views which fall outside the consensus as curious heresies, or, even more effectively, by treating them as irrelevant eccentricities, which serious and reasonable people may dismiss as of no conse-quence"(1969, 220-1).

The critical cultural theory is more concerned in the effect of media messages on society, or groups, rather than the individual. The new approach views the mass media as a cultural industry, whose mission is to produce cultural products. The industry has also a well-developed distribution system. Despite conscious and unconscious efforts to hide the profit motive that drives this industry, like all industries, it does everything legally possible to "improve" its commodity to enhance its profits. As a result, it has always been trying new repacking techniques to better market its product "as entertainment and news, though such "repackaging typically involves considerable distortion which in turn fosters many misimpressions about personal identities and the larger social world." But, the distortions often "provide support for the status quo" (Baran *et al.* 1995, 339).

Critical cultural theory is also "concerned with understanding how elites use media to propagate hegemonic culture as a means of maintaining their dominant position in the social order." Critical cultural theorists argue that the elite class utilize the mass media as a potent instrument to promote their ideology in order to maintain their group interest. Baran and Davis reiterate that the media can be viewed as a public arena in which cultural battles are fought and a dominant or hegemonic culture is forged. Elites dominate these struggles because they start with important advantages.

The way the press marginalizes views different from those of the dominant groups or forces tells the story. The drive to maintain a hegemonic culture involves a systematic suppression of "alternative forms of culture and innovative media use. These theories challenge the power of elite groups by exposing media use and criticizing hegemonic culture . . . .. Opposition is marginalized and the status quo is presented as the only logical, rational way of structuring society" (Baran *et al.* 1995, 281-82).

This perspective, which is frequently used to measure the impact of media messages on social policy and policy making, can explain why the United States institutions of the press and the state become adversaries on domestic issues, but, generally speaking, act as two sides of the same coin on matters relating to foreign affairs. For example, should one assume the same vigilance from the press in its international news coverage as in its domestic coverage? In other words, does the watchdog system, widely practiced at home to keep local, state and federal governments honest, function when covering the news abroad the same way or with the same intensity as at home? Does the element of competition play the same role for a share of the international market as in the domestic market? This interplay of influence—trying to influence each other's agenda—tells only half of the story. The other side shows how these two institutions support each other, especially in times of distress and crisis that threaten the social order. There is no question the pull and push between these two institutions at the domestic level is not evident in the mass media coverage of foreign news.

Several studies show that the difference in the nature of the relationship between the press and the government is evident, even when covering it from Washington. Cohen says, "The prevailing definition of the foreign policy beat as largely bounded by the State Department and Embassy Row has a constraining influence on the choices open to the reporter, and hence, on the conception of foreign policy that he represents to his readers" (1963, 88). This can best be seen in an international story that becomes a "local" one as a result of a high degree of public involvement at home on either side of the issue, an obvious racial dimension to the story, or if there is an extensive United States investment at stake. For example, the American press during the early years of the Vietnam War, by and large followed the official line, and those who tended to question the assumptions of the United States policy and its stated objectives were treated as dysfunctional elements within the press corps. However, this role was reversed after the Tet Offensive of 1968 when television brought the story home and the American people began to realize the futility of the war. As a result, public support of the war efforts showed a marked decline, and criticism of United States policy mounted steadily. The press then went on the offensive and began to be critical of the war and took the White House, the Pentagon, the United States Department of State and other agencies to task. In the process, the press's role of cooperation with the government and its agencies during the early years of the war turned confrontational almost overnight, so much so that, in the end, those on the right of the political spectrum blamed the media "for losing the war," or that it was "lost because of 'liberal' reporting" (Emery and Emery 1988, 519).

Another visible constraint has to do with the news sources that greatly influence the content of news. Many studies have confirmed that American foreign correspondents rely heavily on their embassies and United States Information Agency branches in their works abroad. Welch says, "Reporters get the bulk of their news from State Department handouts, press briefings, informal meetings with State Department officials, and the like" (1971, 225). Among the reasons behind this dependency on official sources are: a) the pressure of deadlines that do not give enough time to gather crucial information independent of official sources; b) lack of expertise to challenge the assumptions behind foreign policy decisions; and c) foreign policy-related news that is mostly initiated by official sources (Welch 1971; Cohen 1963).

Thus, when it comes to covering international news, reporters tend to rely more on information from government agencies than they would when covering domestic stories. But, how does this affect United States press coverage of foreign news? How does this filter down to the editorial and the opinion pages and columns? Sigal says, "What the news is depends very much on who the sources are. If each day's front page were like a single frame in a movie, the composite series of still frames would necessarily contain some distortion . . .. While the camera might belong to newsmen, the lights are in the hands of their sources" (1973, 189).

But this dependency goes both ways. Foreign policy makers also depend rather heavily on the press, especially the elite press, as well as the television networks, to explain policy issues, influence United States legislators, mobilize or fight special interest groups and of course inform constituencies (Noer 1985). The elite press is the only segment of the United States print media involved in direct newsgathering that does not totally depend on the wire services for foreign news. The elite press, as defined in a study conducted by John Merrill nearly a quarter of a century ago, consists of selected newspapers which "are read by the elite . . .. And are aimed at the educated citizen who is aware of, and concerned about, the central issues of his time, and undoubtedly it is read by more opinion leaders than are other types of newspapers" (1968, 7). Thus, the relationship between the American press and the United States foreign policy bureaucracy is generally characterized by interdependency. But, does this interplay between the press and the foreign arm of the United States government extend to the point where the two influence each other's positions on issues? Is there a relationship between the positions of the influential newspapers and official United States stands on foreign policy issues?

Previous studies (Cohen 1963, Malek 1984), which looked into this question in different ways and in different settings, have indicated a strong relationship between the foreign policy arm of the executive branch of the United States government and the press. This book describes and explores this relationship further to determine its nature in the respective positions of the elite press and the United

States government on the issue of national liberation in South Africa, Eritrea and Western Sahara during the period that covers the Carter administration and the first Reagan administration.

In Africa, as in other continents, national liberation movements have represented the outward manifestations of the process of decolonization. The issue of national liberation movements is one of Africa's past and future. C.L.R. James says that a revolutionary national movement "is first and foremost a movement from the old to the new, and needs above all new words, new verses, new passwords— all the symbols in which ideas and feelings are made tangible" (1971, 136).

How the West and the Western press view this issue is very important in our attempt to examine United States policy and attitudes toward the African continent. The history of national liberation movements begins where the history of national oppression starts. But, there is something unique about the post-World War II national liberation movements, which developed within the context of the Cold War. These movements also use protracted guerrilla warfare as the primary tool to achieve their goals. Eqbal Ahmed says, "Occupied nations and oppressed peoples have resorted to guerrilla warfare throughout recorded history. But, only in modern times has it become the acknowledged weapon of the weak, a symbol of our age, registering successes no less than setbacks from China to Cuba, Malaya to Mozambique" (1971, 137).

However, Western reaction to this post-war phenomenon was by and large negative and the movement was viewed, not as a genuine development emanating in response to internal conditions, but as another conspiracy of the then growing communist movement led by the Union of Soviet Socialist Republics. "America's interest in revolutionary warfare began from a counterrevolutionary and defensive posture as a result of reverses in China, Cuba,

Laos—and of its protracted involvement in Vietnam" (Ahmed 1971, 141).

Chapter 2

UNITED STATES POLICY AND
AFRICA'S STRUGGLES FOR FREEDOM

A Policy of Hesitation

The invisibility the United States press "portrays" of Africa today has its roots in the history of United States foreign policy for Africa over the last half century. The legacy of press neglect noted in the previous chapter is a reflection of the United States government's lack of interest in the continent, despite the fact that one of every eight Americans has his or her roots in Africa, the cradle of human kind.

Out of the ashes of World War II came a new global alignment of forces. The end of that war marked more than the humiliating defeat of the Axis powers. It marked the transfer of the mantle of leadership within the western powers from Europe to North America. Wriston puts it this way: "Even the most jaded diplomat might have to concede that the balance of power in the world shifted decisively on July 16, 1945, in the desert of Alamogordo, New Mexico, when the first atomic explosion took place" (1988, 67). The war left European powers too weak and too exhausted to hold on to their colonies in Africa as well as the rest of the Third World. The war created an atmosphere conducive to decolonization "through a number of side-effects and after-effects," as Mazrui (1986) puts it, which, in addition to the weakening of the European colonizers, and the dawning of an independence era in Asia, helped speed up the process of decolonization and brought the issue of the right of the colonized peoples to self-determination to the forefront. The new role as a world leader and the growing "communist threat" forced the United States to pay attention to the continent of Africa, a region it had totally ignored up to this point (Emerson 1958).

This is not to imply that United States-African contact started after World War II. It goes back nearly four centuries to the beginning of the slave trade. The post war contacts, in addition to Washington's perception of itself as a leader of the 'free world,' were based on the public's heightened awareness of foreign affairs created when millions of American troops returned home from North Africa, Europe and other places. However, in most cases there is little or no relationship between the earlier period in United States-African contacts and the one following the war. Emerson (1958) argues that the earlier contacts with Africa are helpful in understanding the nature of United States interests in the continent during the post-war period. The Eurocentric characteristic of the American approach toward Africa did not start in 1945. Nielson states that "American-African relationships through the eighteenth and most of the nineteenth centuries were extremely limited. Militarily, economically, and politically, Africa in American governmental policy was only an adjunct to relationships with Europe" (1969, 245).

But, what was the nature of American interest in Africa during this period? How about United States policy and attitude toward the continent? There is a scattered body of literature that discusses United States African foreign policy

24

during this period which tends to agree on one basic point: that it was full of contradictions between what was stated and what was implemented (Nielson 1969) and that it was consistently characterized by half-hearted moves and lack of ongoing interest toward the continent (Emerson 1958; Ogene 1983; Skinner 1986). Johansen (1980) attributes the contradictions to what he described as America's "dual heritage" in foreign policy: one portrayed in the American desire toward isolationism to maintain its 'innocence,' and the other in which the United States goes all out to maintain its national interests.

Crowder and Oliver (1975) argue that America has been less deeply committed in Africa than in any other part of the world and when it showed some interest it was for reasons that are mostly European. Challenor (1977) believes that one of the many reasons behind this policy of neglect is race. In trying to put the current American behavior and attitude towards Africa within a historical context, she says, "Certain attitudes of United States officials and the citizens were not conducive to favorable policies toward black nations. From the anti-Catholic Know-Nothingism, nativist sentiment, beginning around 1856, the country passed through a period of social Darwinism and bogus anthropological theories about genetic inferiority of the darker races" (1977, 27). She cites United States refusal to recognize Haiti about this time as an equal, sovereign nation, mostly because of the opposition of politicians representing southern plantation states. This issue is of particular importance in assessing historical United States attitude towards black nations because Haitian trade at that time with the United States was more than the combined volume of three South American countries (Argentina, Venezuela and Bolivia), which Washington had recognized.

Duignan and Gann (1984) also add a useful historical background to this conflicting American attitude towards the continent during this period. In *The United States and*

Africa: A History, they write that up until the end of World War II when Washington put the Soviet Union at the top of its enemy list, Roosevelt had fully supported the process of decolonization in Africa. However, after the war, the United States began to rally the European colonizers against the Soviet threat; this, in turn, meant major concessions, on its part, on the decolonization issue.

The *United States Department of State Bulletin,* the official organ of United States foreign policy, an extremely useful source not only for the official position of the government on different African issues but also in assessing the discrepancy between the stated goal and actual implementation of the policy, brings out America's fluctuating attitude toward the decolonization issue. However, the documents, which include all official pronouncements from the president on down, should be taken for what they are: official documents. Such documents are sometimes issued not to reveal but to conceal real intentions behind those pronouncements. For example, as we will see later in the case of Eritrea, while some of these documents talked about "the need to respect the rights of the Eritrean people" (*Bulletin* 22, December 1952), others reveal real United States intentions toward the territory.

Some scholars attribute the American 'policy of hesitation' to Europe being in the way in United States dealings with Africa during these years. In a series of background papers prepared for the 1958 thirteenth annual meeting of the American Assembly, published the same year in *The United States and Africa,* edited by Walter Goldschmidt, a group of elite foreign policy experts provided a useful assessment of how the foreign policy establishment viewed the American strategy toward the continent at the dawn of the independence era. These specialists delved into the politics, economics, and sociology of the continent and its people to urge the United States to get involved in Africa directly and early. They warned against a hands-off policy toward the continent. However, here again, the emphasis was on how best the United States could guide "the free world" and succeed in its strategy of containment, not on how best to help this young continent emerge from nearly a century of European exploitation and degradation. Another very evident characteristic was that the policy was too security conscious to even consider the interests and wishes of the Africans if their needs came in the way of United States military and other foreign policy objectives. The literature shows that it was indeed largely driven by the Cold War.

All in all, the policy had two main characteristics: It was Eurocentric in its perspective and it was driven by the Cold War and, as a result, it was too security conscious to even consider the rights and aspirations of the people, as we will see in the case of Eritrea. This former Italian colony went through one of the most brutal wars in history—and the longest in the history of modern Africa—mostly because of what the United States did during this period driven by Cold War imperatives.

The European Connection and its Cold War Objectives

American national interest in Africa was defined and re-evaluated during the Roosevelt era, and at some point Franklin D. Roosevelt felt that the British imperial system and the monarchy were more of a threat to peace than Marxism-Leninism. Naturally, the British were not exactly enthusiastic about decolonization because they had more to lose than the United States. On the other hand, the United States had nothing to lose and a whole continent to gain. As a result, Washington initially went on a collision course with London on the question of decolonization. Washington wanted a policy that would accelerate the process of "reform" in the colonies and make the weakened European powers accountable to the newly founded United Nations which was soon to be dominated by the United States

(Duignan and Gann 1984). This American position naturally put the European colonizers on the defensive, and the two might have continued on this collision course if the Soviet threat had not become a reality in the form of the gobbling up of Eastern Europe and many other actions taken by the Soviet Union, forcing the United States to reconsider some of its foreign policy objectives and goals. The foreign policy establishment also sounded the alarm about the Soviet threat and began to be concerned about communist influence in the nationalist movements of the continent.

For Africa, this change in the balance of international forces meant a Eurocentric policy, which was less independent than during the war. Skinner argues that the American move was "part of a centuries-long propensity of America's leaders to ignore conditions on that continent or to see them through the prism of European primacy. Then when it appeared that this point of view had to be modified, the United States substituted another prism, that of Soviet Communism, with which to deal with changes that were taking place in Africa" (Skinner 1986, 49). George McGhee, who was the United States assistant secretary of state for Near Eastern and African Affairs during this crucial transition from total neglect and periodic romantic contacts to a security-conscious Cold War foreign policy, described the "so-called colonial powers" in Africa as "our friends and allies" in the global East-West struggle (*Bulletin* June 19, 1950). McGhee made that statement in a speech he delivered before the Foreign Policy Association on May 8, 1950, and made no bones about the United States African policy being totally and unabashedly Eurocentric.

While still emphasizing the need for Africans to be anticommunists, McGhee made it absolutely clear that America was not willing to extend the largess it had shown in its Marshall Plan for Europe to an equally, if not more, needy Africa. The United States, he told the members of the association, was "not in a position to exercise direct responsibility with respect to Africa and has no desire to assume the responsibilities borne by other powers and, indeed, our principles, our existing commitments and our lack of experience all militate against our assumption of such obligations." But, his anti-communist message, "advice" and implied threat to the Africans was as blatant as it could be in his address to the association: "Advantage must be taken of this period of grace to further the development within Africa of heal thy political, economic and social institutions, to create understanding on the part of the Africans of the forces of communism which are disturbing the peace and security of hundreds of millions of people elsewhere in the world, and to inspire a determination to resist these forces" (*Bulletin*, June 19, 1950, 79).

The State Department knew fully well what this meant for Africa, but it had no qualms about reversing itself on the question of decolonization. Emerson (1958) said the United States felt not to consider the European side of the colonial question would have put American interests at risk. The modified United States policy for Africa was essentially a military policy whose main objectives were outside of Africa (Jackson 1982). For example, American strategy in North Africa was chiefly concerned with NATO forces in the Mediterranean Sea or with Middle East related issues.

However, as the decolonization process set in and the era of independence dawned, American policy makers began to look at Africa as an entity separate from Europe— but, not totally independent. As independence loomed, so did the possibility of the new nations hitching their wagons to the Red Star emerging from the East. Naturally, Eisenhower was the first president to have felt the urgency of this possible eventuality. It was not surprising therefore that he sent his vice-president, who was none other than Richard M. Nixon, to represent him at what is considered the official beginning of Africa's era of independence: Ghana's independence celebration in 1957.

Upon his return, the vice-president stressed the growing importance of the emerging continent to 'the free world' and wanted the United States foreign policy establishment to recognize this fact; he recommended that higher priorities be assigned to this region.

Out of this growing concern and attention came one thing that many view as a landmark in United States-African relations: the establishment of a full-fledged Bureau of African Affairs in the United States Department of State. However, even with that, the basis of United States policy towards Africa remained the same throughout the Eisenhower administration. The Eurocentric basis of the policy did not change until the next decade. However, starting in the early 1960s, advances in military technology began to render dispensable the bases that the United States had gone to great length to secure; as a result, Crowder and Oliver (1975) point out, the Kennedy administration promoted a policy that was designed to push France, Britain and Belgium to give up their colonies and transfer power to groups of Westernized elites in the respective African countries. This heralded a new era in the modern history of Africa, the era of neo-colonialism.

The Eritrean Question, Ethiopia and United States Policy

The ambivalence and hesitation that we have seen in the overall United States policy during the early post World War II period was not evident in at least one African issue that the American policy makers faced in the late 1940s. On the Eritrean question, which was part of the issue of the disposal of the three former Italian colonies in the continent, Somalia and Libya being the others, the Americans played an active and consistent role. In a way this was consistent with their Cold War strategy in one corner of Africa. Cliffe (1988), Yohannes (1988), Firebrace (1985) and Sellassie (1980) agree on the two major reasons behind the United

States persistence on this question. Though the Americans already had a military presence in Eritrea during this period, thanks to the British Military Administration that ruled Eritrea from 1942-1952, the State Department felt that the former Italian colony should be linked to Ethiopia in order to ensure a permanent military base in Eritrea.

Furthermore, to these strategists an independent Eritrea would have been an unknown factor in the power equation between the superpowers. Yohannes states that "the United States was not sure how the Eritrean nationalists would react to American military presence in Eritrea in the event that country became independent.... From the standpoint of military strategy, then, it was unwise to risk a future reality which might turn out to be totally against United States military interest there" (1988, 68). The United States and the other powers involved in the disposal of this colony had other options in resolving the question under the United Nations system. Trusteeship to be administered by either the United Nations or Italy was a reasonable option as was recommended for some of the other colonies during a transition period. However, the State Department opposed the idea because such an option would not have achieved the first objective of their position on Eritrea. The U.N. Charter forbids foreign military presence in territories under the trusteeship system.

A third element that played an important part in the United States decision was American interest in Ethiopia and that African country's willingness to play a role as a visible international satellite nation, as was seen in its participation in the Korean and Congo conflicts. Landlocked Ethiopia had its eyes on the prize right from the start and this perfectly coincided with American interest on the Eritrean issue. Ethiopia also used the Cold War to its advantage. In the end, global strategic interests of the United States and a neighbor's need for access to the sea overshadowed the right of the people to determine their own destiny (Firebrace and Holland 1984). These are the three overriding objectives of the policy, but how persistent and consistent were the Americans in implementing the policy?

Except for the initial period before the end of the war, in which the United States was not opposed to the possibility of independence for Eritrea, Washington worked hard to link the Red Sea territory to Ethiopia. Though the British took over Eritrea after the defeat of Italy in 1941, the fate of the former Italian colonies was left in the hands of the Four Powers (the United States, the Soviet Union, France, and Great Britain). Churchill, Truman, and Stalin started discussing the issue in 1945 at the Postdam Conference, but the Four Powers did not take any serious action until two years later. Under a provision in the Peace Treaty with Italy, signed in July 1946, in which Italy was forced to renounce its claims to these territories, the Four Powers established a commission to investigate and find out the wishes and interests of the inhabitants of the former Italian colonies.

However, partly because of maneuvering by the superpowers [the Soviet Union changed its position five times on Eritrea], and partly due to conflicting interests of other parties, the members of the commission, upon their return, could not agree on how to dispose of these territories. However, one thing became very evident right from the start: they were not prepared to base their conclusions and recommendations on what the Eritrean people wanted. Instead, the deadline forced the Four Power Commission of Investigation to refer the matter to the United Nations General Assembly. This was also an action that Washington wanted taken since the U.N. at that time was very much dominated by the United States.

However, as with the Four Powers, when the General Assembly started to discuss the issue seriously on April 6, 1947, it was without the consideration of the views and wishes of the people whose destiny it was determining. In 1949, the Assembly even seriously contemplated a partition proposal for Eritrea, which was rejected left and right by the majority of the Eritrean people and their political parties.

The partition plan was narrowly rejected in the end not because the Eritrean people were opposed to it, but because both Ethiopia and the United States failed to support it. As was indicated above, the United States initially supported the idea for a partition, a plan that would not have jeopardized its objectives since the plan called for that part of Eritrea it wanted as a base to be linked to Ethiopia. The then Secretary of State, Dean Acheson, in a telegram to the American consul in Eritrea, said the United States' position favored union of the eastern part with Ethiopia and the western part to be incorporated into the Sudan. The United States representative at the U.N. also pushed for partition until about six months before the final resolution of the issue. His demand was for "the immediate incorporation of the greater part of Eritrea, excluding the Western Province, to Ethiopia" (*Bulletin,* July 24, 1950, 45). Such an action would be within the United States objectives in the region. However, it later decided to drop the demand because Ethiopia was not in favor of the plan. Korn says that "the United States understood that Haile Sellassie would regard its position on Eritrea as a critical test of friendship" (1986, 1). For Ethiopia, it was not in her interest to back a plan that would limit it to a half of a loaf when the whole loaf was a possibility.

In the next session, the Assembly finally agreed to grant independence to Libya and trusteeship for Somalia for ten years leading to independence. This action made it easier for the State Department to single out the Eritrean question and look for a separate solution. As a result, the world body decided to send another commission of inquiry to Eritrea "to ascertain more fully the wishes and the best means of promoting the welfare of the inhabitants of Eritrea, to examine the question of the disposal of Eritrea and to report to the General Assembly together with such proposals as it may deem appropriate for the solution of the problem with Eritrea (General Assembly Resolution 289-A, 1949; emphasis mine). The commission was also mandated to consider "the rights and claims of Ethiopia…. and the interests of peace and security" (U.N. General Assembly Resolution 390, 1949).

Meanwhile, the State Department went on the offensive, pushing "the incorporation of Eritrea to Ethiopia." However, the American strategy might have been to push the Ethiopian demand to the limit so as to get enough supporters for a federal union plan it had been crafting for some time. The American representative at the U.N., after expressing his government's opposition to independence or trusteeship, and reiterating what he believed to be "the best and most equitable solution" (annexation or incorporation), told the Interim Committee that he was willing "to give careful consideration to a compromise solution involving the federation of Eritrea and Ethiopia under the sovereignty of the Ethiopian Crown" (*Bulletin*, July 24, 1950, 45). By this time, several nations including Italy, Canada and New Zealand went along with the United States.

Eight out of the nine political parties in Eritrea as well as the majority of Eritreans told the second commission what they wanted—independence—but the five members came up with three different solutions ranging from independence to union with Ethiopia. The British administrator in Eritrea at that time criticized the commission for failing to conduct a thorough survey of the political activities and make a credible assessment of how the people felt about the issues that it was sent to investigate (Travaskis 1960). The commission of inquiry did not even consider holding a plebiscite, a well accepted practice by the U.N., "to assess the wishes" of the people.

However, by this time, the State Department had garnered enough votes and the world body by and large ignored the commission recommendations and approved a proposal for a federation under the Ethiopian Crown sponsored by the United States and accepted by Ethiopia.

It must also be noted that Ethiopia played the Cold War card extremely well. During the six months leading to the final resolution of the Eritrean issue, which resulted in stepped-up debate, Emperor Haile Sellassie contributed $100,000 for medical supplies to help the west in Korea, and sent 1100 Ethiopian officers and troops to join the American Seventh Army in Korea (Soany 1951, 1241).

In the end, global strategic interests of the United States and a neighbor's need for access to the sea overshadowed the right of the Eritrean people to determine their destiny. As a result, the annexation process of the former Italian and British colony began in 1952. This total disregard of the opinion of the Eritrean people continued through the next decade when the "federation" stayed in effect, though Ethiopia tried to weaken its provisions every step of the way before it unilaterally abrogated it in 1962. However, by then the armed struggle had begun following a decade of peaceful means of resistance. Eritrean workers, led by the General Union of Labor Syndicates, as well as students staged sporadic strikes to draw attention from the international community, and especially that of the United Nations, which had guaranteed the Eritreans in the final report of the U.N. Commissioner for Eritrea that the federal resolution would not be violated. Even the initial intent of those who started the armed struggle in the fall of 1961, one year before the formal annexation of the territory, with only 13 fighters and 7 antiquated guns, was more to attract U.N. attention than to militarily confront Ethiopia, which had by this time built a well-equipped modern army thanks to a 1953 security pact with the United States. But, that did not happen and, slowly, it became clear to all Eritreans that the only way to regain their national rights as a people was through the barrel of the gun.

As the armed struggle, then led by the Eritrean Liberation Front (ELF), began to gather momentum, Ethiopian reprisals increased in frequency and intensity. The year the Organization of African Unity was founded and established its headquarters in the Ethiopian capital, more than 3,000 Eritreans were jailed because they were suspected of being supporters of the armed struggle. This was a harbinger of the tragedy that was to follow until the war ended almost three decades later with the defeat of the Ethiopian army in May 1991. A killing spree in 1967, which included an indiscriminate aerial bombardment of hundreds of villages, resulted in the first major wave of Eritrean refugees who fled to the Sudan and other countries. Three years later, in another round of reprisals, the Ethiopian army massacred more than one thousand innocent Eritrean civilians in and around the area where ELF fighters had killed an Ethiopian general. This sent another wave of refugees to neighboring nations and other places. This pattern of massive killings, large scale aerial bombardments, forcing thousands more to flee their homes, continued right to the end of the war decades later.

An important political development almost a decade after the first shot was fired to start the armed struggle came in 1970 with the birth of the Eritrean Peoples Liberation Front (EPLF), founded by a group of former ELF members. This proved to be a crucial development in the history of the struggle because the EPLF played a defining role on the rest of the road to liberation. In fact, by the early 1980s, following a tragic civil war, which forced the ELF out of the field and toward virtual disintegration as a major fighting force, the EPLF faced the huge Soviet-armed and advised Ethiopian army alone and, using captured weapons and tanks, built its organization into a formidable military machine. On May 24, 1991, its fighters marched into Asmara, the Eritrean capital, by defeating the huge Soviet-backed Ethiopian army. The Ethiopian defeat in Eritrea, coupled with a series of unprecedented military victories in the spring of 1991 by a coalition of Ethiopian opposition groups forced the Ethiopian president, Mengistu Haile mariam, to flee to Zimbabwe just a few days before the EPLF entered Asmara and brought the entire Red Sea territory under its full control by capturing the second Eritrean port, Assab, on May 25.

Western Sahara, Morocco and United States Policy

The case of Western Sahara, whose roots are traced to 1975 when Morocco tried to annex the territory, was in many ways a repeat of what had happened in Eritrea just 13 years before. Both were annexed during the era of independence by bigger and more populous African neighbors based on "historical" claims with the implicit or explicit blessing of the United States, the main supplier of arms to the annexing nations. In both cases, evidence shows, the actions were taken against the wishes of the peoples of these territories. For example, in 1975 when Spain was about to end its control of the territory, a United Nations Visiting Mission found that "there was a strong consensus among the Saharawis favoring independence and rejecting integration with their neighbors" (Kamil 1987, 19).

For a long time, both Morocco and Ethiopia had annexationist tendencies in their respective regions. For example, in addition to Eritrea, Ethiopia "had also laid claim to Italian Somaliland but this was rejected by the United Nations which returned it to Italy as a Trust Territory in 1950 for a period of ten years" (Sagay and Wilson 1978, 341). Morocco's claims stretched from Mauritania to parts of Algeria and Mali. In fact, Morocco did not renounce its claim over Mauritania until 1970 when the two nations signed a peace treaty.

As in the case of Eritrea, Kamil (1987) argues that United States military support of the annexing nation has played a crucial role in Morocco's decision to take the action. However, in the eyes of most of Africa and the greater part of the rest of the world, the Western Saharan annexation, which took place after the establishment of the Organization of African Unity, the political trend-setter in the continent, is more readily understood and accepted than the Eritrean case.

On February 26, 1976, Spain ended its colonial control of Western Sahara. The next day the Popular Front for the Liberation of Saguia el Hamra and Rio de Oro (Frente Popular para la Liberacion de Saguia el Hamra y Rio de Oro (Polisario)) announced the establishment of a government in exile, the Saharan Arab Democratic Republic (SADR).

Polisario decided to take this immediate step in an attempt to reverse the actions already taken by Morocco and Mauritania and preempt any additional steps that these countries might have in mind to strengthen their control of the territory. A little over three months before, the two neighboring nations were given control over the territory from the departing Spanish colonizers. They formally took over on November 21, 1975, when Spain signed the Treaty of Madrid, ending its colonial hold of the territory and transferring administration to the two neighboring nations, with virtually no participation of the Saharawi people in the deal believed to have been engineered by the then United States Secretary of State Henry Kissinger.

In December 1974, Morocco and Mauritania laid historical claim to the territory, when the International Court of Justice, under a United Nations General Assembly Resolution, looked into the Western Saharan case. The court "found that historical ties did exist in both [the Morocco and the Mauritania] cases but that they were insufficient to establish sovereignty" (Nelson 1986, 283). Even if they had any validity, the court said, "those claims should not negate the right to self-determination of the people of Western Sahara" (Kamil 1987, 18). The two countries partitioned the territory, with Morocco claiming the northern two-third of the territory and Mauritania controlling the remaining one-third. In 1975, Moroccan King Hassan organized a crusade known as the Green March in which 350,000 of his people participated in a long march into the territory, while it was still a Spanish colony, to pressure

Spain to leave the colony so that the two neighboring nations could regain control of the territory.

However, on October 12, 1977, Charles Diggs, then a member of the United States House of Representatives, in the first U. S. Congressional hearing on the Western Sahara conflict, said, "While on the surface the war revolves around territorial claims, in fact the real struggle is over control of the rich phosphate and other mineral resources of this region." He supported the Saharawi people's right to self-determination, and added: "The United States, with its close ties to Morocco, has made our country, in the eyes of some, guilty by association" (Quoted in Kamil 1987, 19).

As in the case of Eritrea, the leaders of Western Sahara see the conflict as a struggle between a people determined to resist subjugation, on the one hand, and, on the other, well-armed neighbors trying to annex this former colony for territorial aggrandizement, its natural resources and to ensure that it is tied to a Western ally in the interest of the East-West struggle for hegemony.

The struggle for self-determination started long before Spain ended its control of the territory but it did not take an armed form until the early 1970s when several guerrilla groups started operations inside what was then Spanish Sahara. Out of these groups emerged Polisario which demanded independence for the territory and set out in May 1973 to achieve it through a protracted armed struggle.

In addition to Polisario, the actors in this struggle are the countries surrounding the territory, Algeria, Morocco and Mauritania. In this lineup of forces, there is a clearly discernible silhouette of the East-West ideological conflict. On the one hand, there were Algeria and Libya, both considered pro-Soviet, supporting the struggle for independence, and on the other hand, there was Morocco, considered pro-West and with a United States supplied and trained armed forces.

Morocco always viewed its pro-Soviet neighbors with suspicion. In fact, Algerian support of Polisario is a reflection and an extension of its hostility toward Morocco. Even though Morocco had given support to the Algerian liberation movement, the two had been on a collision course since the early 1960's when they actually went to war over a border dispute. This animosity between the two nations continued in different forms until the mid-1980s.

The line of demarcation and the East-West dimension to the conflict became clearer in 1979 when Mauritania, with its economy ruined and as a result unable to continue the debilitating war which also led to the overthrow of the regime of Mokhtar Ould Daddah, decided to give up its claim to the territory. The Polisario leadership then decided to intensify their lobbying and diplomatic efforts to gain support of the OAU in order to internationalize the issue and isolate Morocco, though King Hassan had threatened to withdraw from the organization he helped establish in 1963. Polisario soon signed a peace treaty with the new rulers of Mauritania which later recognized the SADR as the sole representative of the people of Western Sahara.

Initially, the OAU attempted to put the issue on hold to find ways acceptable to both sides. In 1982, the majority of the OAU Council of Ministers accepted Polisario's contention and agreed to accept the guerrilla movement as a full member state. However, Morocco managed to get the backing of enough members of the organization to have the annual summit adjourned for lack of a quorum. The next year, the issue divided the organization so much that Polisario decided to "voluntarily" withdraw so that the OAU could hold its annual meeting. But, in the meantime, the movement built up its support within the OAU, and Morocco could not sustain the backing it had in 1982. Eventually, the OAU decided to seat the Saharan Arab Democratic Republic (SADR) as the official representative of the people of Western Sahara.

As expected, Morocco protested the decision and withdrew from the OAU in 1984. However, at this point, support for its claim lost practically all ground in a matter of two years, and, as a result, it stood alone. Zaire voted with it against the well-publicized and well orchestrated proposal introduced to seat the SADR, but Mobutu, whose pro-West regime needed Hassan's intervention in 1978 to survive a serious challenge to its authority, chose not to withdraw from the organization over the Western Saharan case.

The conservative regime of King Hassan tried hard to present the Western Saharan issue in East-West terms, trying to paint the movement as Libyan financed, Algerian directed and Soviet armed, but with very little success. Hassan broke diplomatic relations with Tripoli and tried to isolate Polisario by portraying it as one of Libya's tools in Gadaffi's efforts to overthrow pro-West governments in Africa, especially those closely aligned with the United States. This campaign of mutual distrust, charges and counter-charges between these two Arab nations went on until the early 1980s when they signed a wide-ranging pact which had an adverse impact on Tripoli's backing of Polisario. Algeria, however, was consistent in its support of the struggle and the Saharawi people's right to self-determination, which in 1981 received the backing of the Soviet Union when Algeria brought the Western Sahara case to the United Nations General Assembly.

Where and how does the United States come into this picture? Why is it directly or indirectly involved in this conflict? What is the nature of United States interest in Morocco, in particular, and the region, in general? Relations between the United States and Morocco are traced back to the eighteenth century, but modern contacts did not start until World War II when that country was still a French colony. United States military presence in that Northwest African country predates its independence in 1958 and later increased in both quality and quantity. Military bases that were scheduled to be closed in the early 1960s continued to operate because Morocco began to depend on Washington for military equipment. However, at the beginning of the study period, the Carter administration, as part of the overall United States mood resulting from the Vietnam syndrome, initially refused to approve a request from Morocco for weapons, bombers, helicopters and spare parts. But, that was soon reversed and arms continued to flow once again.

Washington has also looked at Morocco as a moderating influence in the Arab World and in the volatile politics of the Middle East. King Hassan has been a willing surrogate for United States interest in Africa and the Middle East. Two cases can best illustrate this relationship between Morocco and Washington. When a close United States friend, the Shah of Iran, needed a place to flee to from the wrath of his people in 1979, Rabat was willing to give him refuge. A year before, when another United States friend, Mobutu of Zaire, faced one of the strongest challenges to his regime, Hassan sent troops to help his regime.

But, it must be noted that Washington never publicly supported the Moroccan position on the Western Saharan issue. Instead, the United States has backed the demand for a referendum based on an OAU resolution which was also endorsed by the United Nations. The referendum would give the people of Western Sahara the first opportunity in their history to exercise their right to determine their own destiny by allowing them to decide on the question of independence or union with Morocco.

Thus, United States policy on the issue of Western Sahara has been one thing on paper and quite a different thing in practice. In practice, Washington has been Morocco's primary source of arms clearly intended to influence the outcome of the contest for the former Spanish colony, though they were given on condition that they be used only for legitimate defensive and internal security purposes. This support continued at an increased level during the Reagan administration. In fact, the military relationship between Morocco and Washington added a new dimension in 1982 when Rabat agreed to allow the Pentagon to use Moroccan airports for transit flights and emergency operations.

The African National Congress,
South Africa and United States Policy

The political lines of contention as well as the stakes in the South African struggle are clearer than in the Western Saharan and Eritrean cases. Though it is much more complex than what appears to be on the surface, the world sees the South African national liberation struggle as a determined effort by the majority of South Africans, who are black, to overthrow a racist political, economic and social system imposed on the country by a white minority to perpetuate white supremacy, domination and privilege.

South Africa, one of the largest, richest and relatively well developed countries in Africa, has been using its resources and military superiority in the region "to hold the advance of independence and equality" (Woronoff 1979, 276). The efforts to suppress any movement toward freedom and democracy were stepped up during the early post-World War II years, when the white minority sector of the society came to realize that the *process* of decolonization had already begun in Africa and the era of independence was approaching fast.

In the 1948 South African elections, the Nationalist Party came to power on a platform of *apartheid*. The word comes from the party's election slogan, advocating a strict separation of the races. When the Nationalists came to power, what was a party slogan became a national policy and was blessed by the largest Afrikaan church, the Dutch Reformed Church, which gave this abhorrent plan a religious justification. Then the party took a series of political, economical and legal actions to make sure that the races were in fact separate de facto and de-jure. Among the first legal steps taken was the Prohibition of Mixed Marriages Act (1949). This was soon followed by The Population Registration Act (1950), the Group Areas Act (1950), the Prevention of Illegal Squatting Act (1951), the Reservation of Separate Amenities Act (1953), and the Resettlement of

Natives Act (1954), among many other measures, putting the whites in full control over the "Coloreds" and "Natives," transferring practically all arable land to whites and uprooting non-whites whose labor was needed into townships.

Also enacted in 1953 was the Bantu Authorities Act designed to move black South Africans whose labor was not viewed as essential to the mainstream South African economy into "homelands." Under this plan, each of the black South African ethnic groups was to be granted a "homeland," with the whites determining the location, size and degree of "autonomy." The racist regime tried to present these tribal reserves to the South Africans and the rest of the world as "independent" states. Over 85 percent of the land went to the whites who made up less than 20 percent of the population. Thus, the laws of apartheid, elaborately designed to socially, economically and politically control the majority of the population by a racist white minority, affected every aspect of life in South Africa.

This stifling oppression naturally was to trigger an equally extensive and widespread resistance. But, the national liberation struggle in South Africa started long before 1948, though the armed form of the people's resistance was not launched until nearly two decades later. The year 1912, when South Africa's most recognized and oldest nonwhite opposition organization, the African National Congress (ANC), was founded, marks an important landmark in the history of the South African people's struggle to determine their own destiny. The political struggle began as a natural reaction to a system of government that excluded, disenfranchised and brutalized all non-white South Africans. This struggle went through some gruesome stages including the March 21, 1960, massacre outside of the Sharpeville police station in which 69 innocent men and women were killed and 250 wounded after the police indiscriminately opened fire on 5,000 unarmed civilians who were protesting against the racist system of apartheid.

Efforts were also made to fight apartheid in the arena of international public opinion, which seemed to have very little effect at first but, about two decades later, it was to play a crucial role in the final dismantling of the apartheid system. The most important forum that the South African resistance movement used to isolate Pretoria was the United Nations which passed numerous resolutions condemning the racist system and imposing economic sanctions.

Right from the start, the ANC tried to play a pacifist role, advocating the ideals of integration, and tried to build a coalition of all the races and ethnic groups in order to form a truly united front against the policy of white supremacy. For nearly fifty years after its inception, the ANC and other South African opposition groups sought to fight the racist system and achieve fair black representation without resorting to violence—mostly using peaceful marches, protests, and petitions. Nelson Mandela, addressing the Court at his trial on November 22, 1962, said, "Throughout its fifty years of existence the African National Congress... has done everything possible to bring its demands to the attention of successive South African governments. It has sought at all times peaceful solutions for all the country's ills and problems" (1982, 37). These activities increased in intensity after 1948 when the National Party took power and began to implement apartheid. In 1955, the main opposition groups gathered to discuss a common strategy in their fight against the racist system and out of that meeting came the Freedom Charter, which called for the establishment of a democratic South Africa which belonged to all the races. In response, the government arrested more than 150 conference participants and organizers.

However, there were some within the ANC who strongly felt that non-violence, as a primary tool of struggle, had run its course. So, in 1959, massive campaigns organized by the Pan-African Congress (PAC), a radical, ANC splinter group formed a year before, were held to protest the pass-laws. Then came Sharpeville in which hundreds of demonstrators were killed and wounded at the hands of the police forces. These killings raised the political tension in South Africa and, in an attempt to control it, Pretoria imposed a state of emergency throughout the country.

Soon after, the South African regime banned the ANC and PAC, thereby blocking all legal avenues to fight apartheid. That ended the first phase of the anti-apartheid struggle. In 1961, ANC came to the conclusion that non-violence method as a main weapon against an enemy armed to the teeth was not only impractical but also suicidal. It was Nelson Mandela, who had come from within the ranks of the ANC Youth League, "who gave clear and public voice to the widespread feeling that non-military methods of struggle had reached the end of their tether" (Braganca and Wallerstein 1982, 46). At his trial in 1962, Mandela explained to the court why individuals like him were willing to face the brute force that one expects from the racist and oppressive regime in South Africa: "Why knowing all [the risks], knowing in advance that this government is incapable of progressive democratic moves, so far as our people are concerned, knowing that this government is incapable of reacting toward us in any way other than by the use of overwhelming brute force, why I, and people like me, nevertheless, decide to go ahead to do what we must. We have been conditioned to our attitudes by the history which is not of our making....We learned from government of General Smuts at the time of two massacres of our people: the 1921 massacre in Bulhoek when more than 100 men, women, and children were killed, and from the 1923 massacre—the Bondelswart massacre in South West Africa, in which some 200 Africans were killed. We have continued to learn it from every successive government" (Mandela 1982, 38).

Mandela was right when he told the court that government-generated violence can do only one thing: breed counter-violence. A few months later, the ANC formed an armed wing, *Umkonto We Sizwe*. So did the PAC. Both organizations were forced to take these steps in order to meet fire with fire, thus heralding the beginning of the armed stage in the struggle against the minority and racist regime in their country.

The ANC launched the second phase with violent sabotages while transforming the organization abroad to conduct guerrilla activities at home. In a statement issued on June 12, 1964, the day most prominent leaders of the African National Congress—Nelson Mandela, Walter Sisuli, among them—were convicted and sentenced to life in the Rivonia Trial, Albert Lutuli wrote that the ANC "sought every possible means of redress for intolerable conditions, and held consistently to a policy of using militant, non-violent means of struggle. Their common aim was to create a South Africa in which all South Africans would live and work together as fellow-citizens, enjoying equal rights without discrimination on grounds of race, color or creed" (1982, 40).

But, in the end, all avenues of peaceful and non-violent resistance were closed. The African National Congress and other organizations were banned and their leaders were either exiled or thrown in jail. Many of the top leaders had to go underground to continue the struggle. This resistance, in turn, brought more oppression from the racist South African regime, using not only its highly equipped armed forces but also its Parliament which served as the vehicle for making repression legal, and utilizing every weapon of this highly industrialized and modern state to enforce that 'legality,' Mandela said in an appeal to the United Kingdom and the United States, South Africa's 'strongest allies,' to save the jailed ANC leaders and "take decisive action for full-scale action for sanctions that would precipitate the end of the hateful system of apartheid" (1982, 41).

The killings and arrests only fueled the South Africa national liberation movement. In 1976 this added a new dimension when the Soweto uprising increased mass participation and more and more South Africans joined the movement against apartheid. Soweto signaled the beginning of yet another phase of the movement: mass uprising, led by students, in which 176 were killed and more than 1,000 were wounded by police. Though some of the issues that triggered the uprising dealt with schools, the movement soon adopted the demands of the national liberation movement and added a whole new dimension to the anti-apartheid struggle. It must also be noted that the decolonization of neighboring Portuguese colonies of Angola and Mozambique may have given the movement another push and another source of hope.

This development spelled more threat to the state and, as a result, Pretoria unleashed more and more of its coercive power to crush the movement. Anthony Sampson, in one of the latest works on South Africa, *Black and Gold: Tycoons, Revolutionaries and Apartheid*, which he wrote to examine the relationship between politics and multi-national corporations, said that "whatever the failures of apartheid, for a long time it succeeded brilliantly in sweeping the black opposition under the carpet" (1987, 104). To counter the threat that Soweto represented, for example, the army joined the police to put down the uprising, killing more than 600 in the process. One of those killed was Steven Biko, a leader of the Soweto student movement. He died on September 12, 1977, in police detention and a few weeks later all the organizations behind the mass uprising, which started in 1976, were banned.

The new strategy was aimed at raising the consciousness of the people of South Africa as well as influencing international public opinion. One of the key aims of this strategy has been to isolate Pretoria internationally and in all fields of activities, including sports. As was indicated above, starting in the late 1970s, this effort paid off because South Africa's diplomatic, political, economic isolation was to play a very crucial role in the final dismantling of the system of apartheid beginning a decade later.

One recurring theme in the statements from the leaders of the South African movement was an appeal to the

Western powers, especially the United States and Great Britain, to pressure the minority government to release imprisoned ANC leaders and dismantle the abhorrent system of apartheid. However, some of them were critical of the West for doing business with the racist regime in Pretoria in total disregard of the suffering of the majority of its people of South Africa. In 1977, Steven Biko told a Western journalist: "We have no illusions about the African policies of either the United States or the USSR.... Many persons within the liberation struggles look upon the Marxist analysis of repression as the proper diagnosis of their situation. And on top of all this there is the overwhelming evidence of America's involvement in the Third World for the sake of its own economic self-interest. Russia has no investments to protect in Johannesburg. America does" (Sampson 1987, 108).

The United States and most of Western Europe had and still have a special relationship with South Africa, which is highly valued as a source of raw materials for the industrialized western nations including Japan. The United States depends on South Africa for supplies of many key minerals. For example, the United States depends on this African country for nearly 90 percent of its chromium imports. Other crucial minerals that come out of that region are manganese, chromite, vanadium and platinum (Adelman 1980, 22). Western Europe and Japan's dependency on South African minerals is even higher. Adelman says, "The vast majority of all EEC [European Economic Community] mineral imports from Africa come from South Africa... Europe and Japan lack the strategic stockpiles held by the United States.... Europe and Japan would be far more adversely affected by a cutoff of the South African supply than would the United States" (1980, 24). Coupled with this are United States economic ties as well as geopolitical considerations which include keeping the Cape route under the control of a regime that Washington trusts, mostly for United States military reasons.

Another important United States interest is the democratization of the region. Because of the racial dimension to the conflict, a democratic state would assure the West permanent access to South African resources. Bloomfield believes that the democratization objective should be the overriding American interest in South Africa. He says, "The principal and overriding United States interest in South Africa is the existence of a state in which non-whites have full civil and political rights" (1988, 213). Many do not believe that this was in fact the overriding United States objective in South Africa, and the United States government began to feel the pressure during the study period to change its South African policy. In the United States, many African-American organizations, most notably TransAfrica and the NAACP (the National Association for the Advancement of Colored People), began to openly challenge the policy through sit-ins, demonstrations and other non-violent methods. Thus, Africa's voice at the United Nations and Black America's political clout at home were factors that the successive American administrations had to consider in their African policymaking process. And as a result of the persistent pressure that came about globally and from within the United States, South Africa and its apartheid policy became an American election issue beginning the second half of the 1970s and throughout the 1980s. But, it must be noted that, despite those mounting pressures both at the United Nations and at home, Washington continued to do business with South Africa.

* * *

In conclusion, it can be stated that America's attitude and policy of ambivalence and hesitation may have prolonged the completion of the decolonization processes and final liberation of the continent and its people. This becomes even clearer in our subsequent chapters, which discuss the interplay of influence and support between the government and the press in a more specific terms.

Chapter 3

WHAT THE RECORDS SHOW: THE DOCUMENTS

With the arrival of the Carter administration in 1977, it appeared that a dramatic shift was to take place. The new president came in advocating the removal of the racist apartheid policy of South Africa and the attainment of a majority rule in that country became a priority goal of American policy for the continent. Unlike United States foreign policy for Africa during the previous United States administrations characterized by almost total neglect of the continent, until the mid 1970s when the Soviet Union began to project its power in Africa in a way and to a degree never seen before, the Carter presidency started off with a policy that made many explicit and implicit promises of change in Africa—both symbolic and real efforts to preempt the communist threat diplomatically.

Part I of this chapter takes a close look at the official foreign policy records as documented in the *United States Department of State Bulletin* during the study period to examine American policy during the Carter years and the first term of the Reagan presidency. Part II examines how the two designated elite newspapers viewed the African policies of the two American administrations.

The First Period (1977-1980)

More than the administrations before and after it, the Carter presidency put a great deal of focus on Africa. "I think it's accurate to say that never before in the history of our nation have we shown any substantial interest in the continent of Africa," said Jimmy Carter who became the first American president in the history of the United States to make an official visit to a black African nation (*Bulletin,* July 1978, 21). President Kenneth Kaunda of Zambia, in an exchange of toasts at a state dinner at the White House three months after the new administration took office, attributed the new African approach to Carter's upbringing: "Jimmy Carter's background has greatly assisted America's approach to Africa and the Third World. Africa today is much higher on the list of American priorities. This is not a favor to Africa. It is simply the result of an honest facing of realities in the maintenance of international peace and security....[In southern Africa] there is greater understanding and acceptance that the interests of the United States of America will not be served by the status quo but a change in structural relations between white, black, and brown, in which no one race will be superior over the others (*Bulletin,* July 1978, 34).

There was widespread recognition that the status quo was no longer able to serve the political and economic interests of the United States in Africa. However, the most important factor that prompted Washington to put the spotlight on Africa was the increasing pace of radicalization of the region. Carter said, "In the past, we've not had an adequate interest there. And almost by default, because we came in late or because we were not involved in a friendly, normal trade relationship where mutual trust and mutual friendships existed, we saw those countries turning to

Marxist countries or Eastern countries for their support and their friendship" (*Bulletin,* July 1978, 19).

Carter and his foreign policy officials were constantly criticized, especially by those who were accustomed to an Eurocentric approach which saw the continent as an adjunct of Europe, for "being preoccupied" with Africa. The documents show that the media raised the question of whether the administration was not putting too much emphasis on Africa. As a result, Carter and the members of his foreign policy team had to constantly justify why Africa was important to the United States.

Right from the start, the foreign policy makers of the new administration tried to define the policy, some of the key elements of which were continued from that of the Ford administration, put in place by Henry Kissinger in 1976 in response to Soviet power projection into the continent. However, despite the refreshingly new attitude toward the continent, the building up and articulation of the new policy was slow. In fact, three months into the new presidency, the *Washington Post*, in an editorial aptly entitled "What is Our African Policy?" accused the administration of "allowing individuals like Andrew Young to improvise policy on the basis of personal predilections" and warned that "there is a real danger here of running off the rails if the administration does not slow down, figure out a policy that is at once responsible and feasible and likely to secure a solid domestic underpinning, and explain it clearly, first at home" (May 1977, 76).

However, slowly, the documents show, the policy took a definitive shape and President Carter best articulated it during his historic trip to Africa in early 1978. He began to set his administration's foreign policy priorities almost one year before his African visit. In his March 17, 1977 speech at the United Nations, he crystallized his African policy into a three-point plan which he described as being consistent not only with American "historic values and commitments," but also "consonant with the ideals of the United Nations" (*Bulletin,* April 1977, 333).

The objectives became clearer as the administration began to look a little harder at the national interest that motivated American policy makers to look at Africa a little closer. Three months later, Secretary of State Cyrus Vance, in his address to the annual convention of the NAACP was more candid and realistic in his assessment of their foreign policy objectives. He cited several political, economic and strategic reasons behind Washington's renewed interest in Africa. "The success or failure of the search for racial justice and peace in southern Africa will have profound effects among the American people," Vance said, and added that:

- The African nations, which constitute one-third of the United Nations member nations, play a pivotal role in that world body.
- Africa accounts for 38 percent of United States crude petroleum imports. Add to that "Africa's mineral and agricultural wealth already provides a substantial portion of our imports of such commodities as copper, cobalt, and manganese for our homes."
- That American direct investment and trade in sub-Sahara Africa went up sixfold and nearly tenfold during the previous decade and half (*Bulletin,* August 1977, 166).

However, the geopolitical considerations in United States foreign policy were not mentioned. In fact, as we will see below, the Soviet Union and its actions in Africa, as elsewhere in the world, displayed an unprecedented projection of Soviet power into the Third World during this period, and, in many cases, this determined the extent and duration of United States attention that a region or country received. However, explaining the general nature of the United States' approach to meet these objectives, Vance said, the best course in American foreign policy is not to counter a foreign power but to remove the reasons that necessitated such an intervention (*Bulletin,* August 1977, 166).

Once again, the policy was best articulated by the President himself almost a year after his foreign policy team began to put the pieces together into a coherent plan. In a statement in Lagos, Nigeria, on April 1, 1978, Carter cited three factors that shaped his administration's policy toward Africa:

- "A commitment to majority rule and human rights";
- "A commitment to economic growth and human development";
- "A commitment to an Africa that is at peace, free from colonialism, free from racism, free from military interference by outside nations, and free from the inevitable conflicts that can come when the integrity of national boundaries are not respected."

Carter told the then Nigerian President, Lt. General Olusegun Obasanjo, that "these three common commitments shape our attitude toward your continent" (*Bulletin,* May 1978, 12).

As to how best to implement the plan and meet the challenge of the Soviet Union's unprecedented projection of power into Africa, the foreign policy team was badly divided. Vance, apparently responding to arguments put forth mainly by National Security Adviser Zbigniew Brzezinski, who advocated a show of force to meet the Soviet challenge in Africa, said, "A negative, reactive American policy that seeks only to oppose Soviet and Cuban involvement in Africa would be both dangerous and futile" (*Bulletin*, August 1977, 166). Eventually, Vance's approach was adopted and used as the main guide in implementing the new policy. The basic approaches were based on the following assumptions:

- That affirmative policies are the most effective;

- That actual assistance to Africa determine long-term success of United States policy toward the continent;
- That any attempt to impose solutions that adversely affect African nationalism would not be accepted;
- Reflecting America's national values, these policies should support peaceful resolution to the racial crisis in southern Africa;
- These policies should promote openness and, thus, the United States must be willing to talk to all, including those who disagree with American policy toward Africa.

To show the degree of its commitment to change in Africa, and as a result of it, the administration supported efforts to repeal the then six-year old Byrd Amendment, under which the United States imported chrome from what was then Rhodesia, defying a U.N. Security Council decision. Carter viewed the measure as central to his African policy. The administration also increased economic assistance from $271 million in 1976 to $450 million in 1978 and encouraged the Western European nations to do the same. The increase was essentially in two developmental areas: The Sahel Fund and a special fund earmarked for southern Africa.

Also significantly different in Jimmy Carter's approach, compared to those of the administrations before and after his, was that African-Americans were given a chance to play a central role in the making and implementing of his African policy. Carter appointed Andrew Young as United States representative to the United Nations and in that capacity Young became one of the key individuals responsible for the new administration's African policy. President Carter attributed the development and implementation of his African policy to Vice-President Walter Mondale, and Secretary of State Cyrus Vance as well as to Ambassador Andrew Young. Also playing a crucial role was Carter's National Security Advisor Brzezinski. A few weeks after Carter's inauguration, the president sent Young on a 17-day

African tour to gather information on which to base United States policy toward the continent. Young also made some other trips to Africa within the first few months. In fact, he was criticized by detractors for putting too much focus on Africa. Praising the contributions both United States Ambassador Andrew Young and Donald McHenry—who started as United States Deputy Representative to the U.N. Security Council and later became ambassador to the U.N.—had made to the American effort to bring about independence and freedom to Namibia and Zimbabwe, President Carter said change in South Africa would also directly affect how America conducts its foreign policy. "It affects not only how we conduct our foreign policy but the way we use the talents of all Americans in our work here and abroad. The diversity of our society is one of its greatest strengths. That diversity must be reflected—to a greater degree than in the past—at all levels of the Department of State" (*Bulletin,* March 1979, 43).

The components of the new American policy on Africa differed among South Africa, Eritrea/Ethiopia, and Western Sahara/Morocco, three case studies that represented the last and most difficult stage of the decolonization process in Africa.

SOUTH AFRICA

Practically all of the foreign policy officials who spoke for the Carter administration said that Africa had increasingly become important to the United States. But, there was no question that the tension in southern Africa played a crucial role in drawing Washington's close attention to the continent. South Africa loomed large in practically all of the key goals of American policy toward Africa during the study period, though the Carter and Reagan administrations had different focus areas during their respective years in office. Richard Moose, Carter's Assistant Secretary for African Affairs, speaking at Yale University, explained why:

"Within the past two years southern Africa has been pro-pelled into the front ranks of United States policy con-cerns....because the region is undergoing fundamental, irre-versible political change—and the pace is accelerating. *At the heart of this process is racial conflict*....Stock assump-tions, widely held in the past, such as the survivability of the minority white regimes, have been quickly, even sud-denly, cast aside" (*Bulletin*, October 1979, 20; emphasis mine).

As soon as Carter became president, the South African case took a new dimension. The goal of achieving social justice and majority rule was defined by the administration as "one of the great moral and political issues of our time" (*Bulletin*, April 1977, 318). The issue was also part of Carter's human rights campaign. The new president's com-mitment to human rights required a strong opposition to racist policies of South Africa. "A policy toward southern Africa that is not firmly grounded on this principle [human rights] would be inconsistent with our national character and therefore would not command the support of the American people. Moreover, it would cast doubt on our commitment to social justice both here at home and else-where in the world," said Philip Habib, Under Secretary for Political Affairs, in a testimony before the Subcommittee on Africa (*Bulletin,* April 1977, 318-319).

A closer look at the *Department of State Bulletin* records for the period of this study, therefore, brings out the following themes in Carter's South African policy: majori-ty rule, human rights, economic sanctions, developing black moderate leadership, and communism. Some of these issues did not crystallize until the implementation of the policy was underway. One of these was economic sanctions.

Majority Rule

This aspect of the policy referred not only to South Africa, but also to Rhodesia (Zimbabwe) and Namibia. Secretary of

State Vance explained clearly how the three southern African issues were intertwined. "Some have argued that apartheid in South Africa should be ignored for the time being, in order to concentrate on achieving progress on Rhodesia and Namibia," Vance said in his remarks to a NAACP convention. But, he added, a policy that would compromise on the question of social justice in South Africa would not only be wrong, but also it would not work (*Bulletin,* August 1977, 168).

However, since Zimbabwe and Namibia are outside of the scope of this study, the issue will be examined only within the context of South Africa because the central point was and still remains apartheid, the dismantling of which was viewed as indispensable for achieving majority rule in this troubled African country. The majority of the official records as well as the editorials in the two elite newspapers focused on apartheid more than on any other policy issue during this period. Though both administrations continually expressed abhorrence to apartheid, there was a marked difference in their respective approaches to bring about majority rule. The Carter administration believed in exerting maximum pressure on the racist, minority regime in Pretoria to accept the principle of majority rule, while Reagan thought a 'constructive engagement' with the South African regime would produce the intended result.

In the beginning, the documents show Pretoria was polite and diplomatic in its reaction to the American attention to apartheid. However, the white minority regime soon began to criticize the Carter policy as being "threatening and punitive." In fact, later Prime Minister Vorster characterized Carter's policy as "strangulation by finesse" (*Bulletin,* October 1977, 446).

Responding to some of the charges, Carter, in a group interview with members of the Magazine Publishers Association, said, "We are not trying to overthrow their government, but we do feel that there ought to be some equality of hiring practices, equality of pay for the same kind of work done, promotion opportunities for black citizens—which is not there—an end to the highly discriminatory pass system that exists in Africa" (*Bulletin,* July 1977, 47). Mondale, after a two-day meeting with Vorster in early 1977 in Geneva, was very blunt about the need for some visible development on the three related issues listed by Carter, in Zimbabwe, Namibia and South Africa itself. In a press conference following the meeting, Mondale said, "We were anxious at the same time that this meeting be one in which we could very clearly define American policy and further make clear the depth and the permanence of our commitment to human rights as a central element in our relations with the government of South Africa and as a policy guiding our affairs in southern Africa" (*Bulletin,* June 1977, 663). The main thrust of the vice president's message to the South African government was that intransigence or delay in bringing about majority rule in Rhodesia and Namibia and a visible progress toward the same goal in South Africa itself was an invitation for the Soviet Union to interfere in this already highly tense region. "They know that we believe that perpetuating an unjust system is the surest incentive to increase Soviet influence and even racial war but quite apart from that is unjustified on its own grounds.... [If Pretoria fails to make these changes,] we would take steps true to our beliefs and values.... For a failure to make progress will lead to a tragedy of human history" (*Bulletin,* June 1977, 663).

Other United States officials also did not mince words in warning Pretoria to reassess its views and stances on the three interrelated questions in southern Africa. Among them was Ambassador Andrew Young who told participants to the International Conference in Support of the Peoples of Zimbabwe and Namibia in Maputo, Mozambique, May 16-21, 1977, that change in South Africa "must begin now" (*Bulletin,* July 1977, 56). Brzezinski also was very persistent without being dictatorial: "I don't think we should be dictating the nature of the change... [However], the pace of that change has to be rapid enough to anticipate international pressures and internal pressures... [Because] once urban violence develops, once there is major intrusion of foreign influence and support, the situation becomes increasingly uncontrollable" (*Bulletin,* December 1977, 800). Such a situation would prevent United States policy makers from implementing their policy of moderation and even tempt the Soviet Union to "exploit" the crisis.

Richard Moose, in a statement before the Subcommittee on Africa of the House Committee on International Relations on October 26, 1977, put this delicate issue this way: "We are not trying to tell South Africa what to do.... We have, however, made it clear that it would be increasingly difficult for the United States to maintain the relationship it has had with South Africa.... Let me emphasize that our policy is not threatening or punitive, as some in South Africa have stated.... We did not lay down a threat to the South African government. We posed it a choice" (*Bulletin,* December 1977, 898). Even after imposing a mandatory sanctions, American policy makers continued to describe their approach as one of communication and persuasion.

However, at the end of the first year of Carter's presidency, there was little movement on practically all the issues, but especially majority rule. Vance, in his summary report of the first year, still steered between two extreme positions, one of which advocated strong pressure and isolation of the South African government. Other forces argued in favor of ignoring apartheid for the time being in return for South African cooperation in the resolution of both the Zimbabwean and Namibian cases. Vance reiterated that the United States had only limited leverage to effect change in South Africa. "But we are among the few governments in the world that can talk to both white and black Africans frankly and yet with a measure of trust" (*Bulletin,* February 1978, 24). The American policy makers were convinced that "we believe that we can effectively influence

61

South Africa on Rhodesia and Namibia while expressing our concern about apartheid" (*Bulletin,* February 1978, 25).

At the end of 1978, or half way into the Carter presidency, there was very little impact of the American effort on Pretoria. James F. Leonard, acting United States Representative to the United Nations, in a statement in the General Assembly on November 22, 1978, admitted that the United States policy makers were still "looking anxiously for signs of... progress.... We look to South Africa for signs that it will cease bannings and detentions without charge; abolish the pass laws and all other forms of discrimination; give an equal opportunity to all for employment, job promotion, and education; and provide for the full political participation of all its citizens, regardless of race or color" (*Bulletin,* February 1979, 61). Six months later, Richard Moose, speaking at Yale University, said that, though the initial intention was to bring about a peaceful change in South Africa, "the key issue today [April 18, 1979] is not whether the changes we now see unfolding will be peaceful or violent, but whether there is still a change to render less violent the inevitable transition to majority rule" (*Bulletin,* October 1979, 20).

Human Rights

On the question of human rights, an issue of extreme importance to the Carter administration, again South Africa dominated the headlines and editorial space during this period. The documents show that the foreign policy team as well as the president and vice-president made it clear the issue of human rights was indeed at the heart of their African policy. Mondale, in his meeting with Vorster talked about "the depth and permanence" of the Carter administration's commitment to human rights and how central that was to United States-South African relations (*Bulletin,* December 1977, 846). In the eyes of the administration, South Africa stood alone from a human rights point of view. William Maynes,

Assistant Secretary for International Organization Affairs, in an annual assessment of the United Nations, said, " In the wake of the Holocaust, never again could the world permit millions of people to be judged legally by their fellow countrymen on the basis of the color of their skin or their ethnic origin, as opposed to their individual actions or political beliefs. It is in this respect, and this respect alone, that South Africa stands apart in the world and must be judged apart.... A failure, therefore, to see what is at stake in South Africa connotes a moral blindness that ignores the past and misreads the future" (*Bulletin,* January 1979, 48).

Economic Sanctions

The United States Department of State defined economic sanction as "an action toward another nation intended to force it into a desired course" (*Bulletin,* March 1978, 22). The department said that the threat of economic sanctions "encouraged American firms doing business in South Africa to improve working conditions for their black employees." William E. Schaufele Jr., Assistant Secretary for African Affairs, in his remarks before the American Academy of Political and Social Science, said such an action by American multinational corporations "could be a significant American contribution to the principle of social justice and provide a vehicle for promoting economic and social progress" (*Bulletin,* May 1977, 469). But, the administration and the elite press resisted the drive for economic sanctions against South Africa right from the start.

However, following the death of Steven Biko on October 19, 1977, and a widespread crackdown which resulted in the arrest of many black leaders, the United States and the rest of the Western nations which had been working on the three key southern African issues reacted strongly and supported a mandatory arms embargo. United States Ambassador to the United Nations Andrew Young, in the Security Council, said, "My government has reluctantly but firmly concluded that the international community must now take steps to insure that the flow of arms into South Africa does not add to a level of tension which is already endangering international peace. My government therefore is prepared to join with others in supporting Security Council action to establish a mandatory arms embargo under Chapter VII of the U.N. Charter" (*Bulletin,* December 1977, 859). In his assessment of the 32nd United Nations Assembly, Young hailed the embargo as an "historic step forward by the United Nations in its long effort to achieve freedom and human dignity in Africa" (*Bulletin,* February 1978, 53). Stung by criticism that it did not try to stop arms traffic to South Africa, the administration went before the Subcommittee on Africa of the House Committee on International Affairs, to defend its arms embargo policy toward South Africa which was a continuation of policy put in place in 1962 to ensure that Pretoria did not get weapons it could use to enforce its racist system of apartheid (*Bulletin,* September 1977, 320-322).

During the last year of the Carter presidency, the Department of State was more willing to impose economic sanctions to force South Africa to change its racist policies. William Dunfey, Alternative Representative to the U.N., in an address to the 34th U.N. General Assembly, at the end of the third year of the Carter years in the White House, said, "We believe that economic forces are particularly important in an effort to effect the kinds of changes in South Africa we all desire" and went on to explain what Washington had done and was planning to do to bring about those changes in that southern African country. In addition to backing a mandatory arms embargo in the Security Council, the United States unilaterally imposed a ban "on all exports of whatever nature to the South Africa military and police" and "urged United States firms operating in South Africa to institute, maintain, and expand enlightened employment practices for their black employees, including improve-ments in wages, working conditions, fringe benefits, and opportunities for advancement, as well as dealing with legitimate representatives of black workers, including black unions" (*Bulletin,* April 1980, 66). But, the administration continued to oppose the idea of American companies divesting themselves of all stocks in firms doing business in South Africa.

Developing Moderate Leadership

This part of the policy had two purposes: to find a "moderate" alternative leadership to that of the national liberation movement and to show black South Africans that armed struggle was not the way to bring about justice. Brzezinski said that the two main goals of United States policy makers were "to create a situation of relative moderation and progressive accommodation" (*Bulletin,* December 1977, 802).

In their effort to line up support within Africa, Washington's policy makers had always tried to establish and strengthen contacts with "moderate" African leaders, "moderate" African nations in the respective crisis areas, as well as Western Europe and South Africa itself. However, the development of the so-called moderate leadership, especially in South Africa loomed very large in Carter's policy. The issue of finding alternative leadership to those of the national liberation movements was at the center of the American strategy. Within the first few months of his presidency, Carter invited Gathsha Buthelezi, leader of the Zulu tribe and the Inkatha Party, who opposed the South African liberation movement led by the ANC. Other such leaders in the region were Joshua Nkomo, president of the Zimbabwe African People's Union, and Bishop Abel Muzorewa, chairman of the United African National Council. However, the leader who the United States policy makers believed had the key to the main problems of the region was South African Prime Minister John Vorster. Vice-President Walter Mondale met Vorster in Vienna in May of that year when Mondale went to Spain, Portugal, Yugoslavia and England "to pursue as effectively as possible additional foreign policy objectives that are also central to the goals of my administration," said Carter in a statement he put out to explain the vice president's 12-day trip to Europe (*Bulletin,* June 1977, 659).

The documents show that though some officials were not opposed to the use of the term or the idea of "liberation" or even "liberation forces," American policy makers were universally opposed to armed struggle as a means to achieving such liberation. This comes out in almost all the relevant documents. Andrew Young, for example, in his address at the Maputo Conference, said, "the armed struggle..., though its final outcome is inevitable, exacts a cruel price from the people of Zimbabwe and Namibia. Africa needs the leadership that will be lost in a prolonged struggle; it needs the infrastructure that will be destroyed in extended military conflict. This is why one objective of this conference should be to make it clear that U.N. members, as always, prefer a negotiated settlement where it can be found." However, he emphasized, "the goals of freedom and liberation are fundamental in the Carter administration's approach to the issues of southern Africa. It is seeking appropriate ways to promote these goals through the aggressive pursuit of negotiated settlements" (*Bulletin,* July 1977, 55-58).

Speaking a few months later at the United Nations-sponsored World Conference for Action against apartheid in Lagos, Young reiterated his position against armed struggle. "I don't believe in violence. I fought violence in my own country.... Too often, however, the armed struggle is advocated most vigorously by those who are thousands of miles away and those whose only contribution to the struggle is the rhetoric of bitterness and frustration." However, he added, "I have never condemned another man's right to take up arms in pursuit of his freedom" (*Bulletin,* October 1977, 447). At the end of a five-day conference, the Lagos World Conference issued a declaration condemning apartheid but also supporting the armed struggle against the racist system. The 34-point declaration was adopted by consensus, but with reservations by the United States.

President Kenneth Kaunda of Zambia, in remarks during his state visit to the United States in May 1978, even tried to explain the goals of the liberation movements, which he said were the same as those of the American Revolution 200 years before. "The same spirit and beliefs contained in the American Declaration of Independence motivate liberation movements. They want freedom and independence" (*Bulletin,* July 1978, 34). President Carter, in a joint communiqué with Nigerian President Lt. General Obasanjo, was given another chance to show support for the national liberation movements in South Africa. However, the communiqué attributed that support to only the Nigerian head of state.

The administration also solicited full participation of the rest of the continent and its leadership to prevent further radicalization of the continent and diplomatically preempt Soviet efforts in the region. The administration was aware of its limitations. It knew from the start that if any solutions were to come, the continent of Africa would have to get fully involved. It also urged the developed countries of Europe and Asia, which had important interests in this region, to get involved in the search for a just solution. But, it kept ignoring the ANC. United States policy makers never considered South Africa's main liberation movement as a potential contributor to a solution in that troubled African country. This is in line with Washington's attitude toward the national liberation movements, which have generally been viewed as part of the problem, if not the problem that the policy makers work to "solve."

Communism (Soviet-Cuban Intervention)

Probably the most important ingredient in Carter's African policy, as in those of the administrations before it during the second half of this century, was opposition to communism and Soviet intervention. One of the principal goals of the policy was to reverse and prevent further radicalization of the continent using policy instruments that combined both competition and confrontational tactics. The issue of communism came up in the documents in different ways ranging from Cuban surrogate troops to East European interests on the continent. Richard Moose said, "When we speak of communism in Africa, we are speaking almost exclusively of the role of the Soviet Union, the Eastern European countries under Soviet domination, Cuba, and, to a much lesser extent, China" (*Bulletin,* December 1979, 29).

Initially Carter favored a less confrontational response. "We do more harm than good by dramatizing the East-West factor.... When we look at African questions as East-West rather than African in their essential character, we are prone to act more on the basis of abstract geopolitical theorizing than with due regard for local realities," said a member of the foreign policy team (*Bulletin,* December 1977, 843). Later on, however, the administration was more willing to apply force to effect change. Carter, in an interview with foreign correspondents, said, "I believe that unless we let a clear signal go to the Soviet Union that we allies stand united in not only condemnation of this action but that we are going to take firm actions to show the Soviets that they will suffer because of it, that might lead to increasing encroachment by the Soviet Union against other countries." However, this change in Carter's attitude towards the Soviet Union and his willingness to use American military muscle to counter their power projection into the Third World has to do more with their invasion of Afghanistan than with their actions in Africa. Soon after the invasion, Carter said on national television: "My opinion of the Russians has changed more drastically in the past week than in the previous three years" (*Bulletin,* June 1980, 14). Toward the end of his presidency, Carter went even further and stressed what he had totally ignored the first two years of his presidency: militarism. Though the invasion of Afghanistan was the primary reason behind this change of heart, there is no doubt it affected his African policy.

ERITREA/ETHIOPIA

United States policy makers also showed increasing concern about the growing crisis in the Horn of Africa. Carter himself, in a speech to representatives to the United Nations General Assembly on March 17, 1977, eight weeks into his administration, identified the Horn of Africa as one of the four major regions that required United States attention. The other regions were the Middle East, Southern Africa and the Eastern Mediterranean area. About ten weeks later, he repeated his belief that the Horn of Africa was in fact a potential trouble spot in the continent. "The other part of Africa that we are quite concerned about…is in the Horn of Africa with Somalia and Afars and Isas, Ethiopia, Sudan, and to some degree Ethiopia on the southern part of the Red Sea and, of course, the Arab countries to the north. But we are working closely there with the Saudi Arabians in particular…. trying to understand the conflict within Ethiopia concerning the Eritreans. That is where the potential trouble spot is in Africa" (*Bulletin,* July 1977, 48).

However, the one issue that almost totally preoccupied United States policy for the region was not the growing Eritrean-Ethiopian conflict or even the Ethiopian-Somali dispute, but the Soviet/Cuban intervention. The intervention in the Horn of Africa put United States policy toward Soviet expansion in the Third World to a test.

Communism (Soviet-Cuban Intervention)

The situation in the Horn of Africa, which was not any less fluid and fast moving than that in the southern part of the continent, also forced the Carter administration's immediate attention to the Soviet threat. The new Ethiopian regime asked Washington to reduce the number of personnel and eventually close the American communications station in Asmara, Eritrea. The Eritrean liberation movement also intensified its activities throughout the Red Sea territory. All signs also indicated a massive Soviet intervention along with its satellites, especially Cuba and East Germany.

In early 1978, a few weeks before Vance's visit to Moscow, President Carter said that "the projection of Soviet power into Africa was a very ominous trend," and Henry Kissinger added that "another move of the kind we have seen in Angola and Ethiopia will raise the presumption that we are facing a global geopolitical challenge incompatible with any definition of detente" (*Bulletin,* June 1978, 29).

The administration's top foreign policy officials were divided over how to respond to the Soviet-Cuban intervention in the Horn of Africa. The majority continued to prefer inaction, while some, especially Brzezinski, advocated a strong action including sending aircraft carriers as close to the region as possible. Carter leaned toward the faction within the foreign policy team that advocated a less confrontational way of responding to the communist challenge in the region and the rest of the continent, citing three factors that would prevent the Soviet-Cuban intervention from succeeding: African nationalism, Soviet racism and communist atheism. "An innate racism that exists toward black people within the Soviet Union, as compared to us" and Africans' "strong sense of religious commitment," he said, would stop Moscow's power projection into the continent (*Bulletin,* July 1978, 21).

But it was Secretary of State Vance who strongly and consistently argued against interjecting into this multifaceted conflict: "The history of the past 15 years suggests that efforts by outside powers to dominate African nations will fail. Our challenge is to find ways of being supportive without becoming interventionist or intrusive" (*Bulletin,* August

1977, 169). He said the danger of unrestricted arms transfers "is particularly great in the Horn, where there has been
an escalation of arms transfers from the outside," and criticized the Soviet Union for doing exactly that. However, he
said, "in accordance with the policy recently announced by
the president, arms transfers to Africa will be an exception-
al tool of our policy and will be used only after the most
careful consideration" (*Bulletin,* August 1977, 169-70).
However, the United States ambassador to the United
Nations did not seem to show too much concern about the
Soviet Union or Cubans. In his assessment of the 32nd
United Nations General Assembly, for example, the danger
of Soviet and Cuban actions in both Eritrea and Ethiopia
that year did not figure in his report.

As stated above, the documents show that the administration was badly divided on how to deal with the Soviet-led
intervention in the Horn and the rest of Africa. But slowly,
even the dominant faction on the foreign policy team which
pushed for less confrontational tactics began to show irrita-
tion. Vance, in a testimony before the Subcommittee on
African Affairs of the Senate Committee on Foreign
Relations, said: "We have told the Soviets and Cubans, publicly and privately, that we view their willingness to exacerbate armed conflict in Africa as a matter of serious concern"
(*Bulletin,* July 1978, 31).

But, the administration was consistent in sounding
warning that Soviet-Cuban military intervention in Eritrea
would result in more killings. Carter, speaking in Lagos,
Nigeria, on April 1, 1978, said: "We are concerned that foreign troops are already planning for military action inside
Ethiopia against the Eritreans, which will result in greatly
increased bloodshed among those unfortunate peoples"
(*Bulletin,* May 1978, 14). He repeated this warning on
another occasion during his African trip, which took him to
Nigeria and Liberia. The American president also asked the
African countries to find peaceful solutions to the conflicts
in the Horn of Africa. Vance said, "We support very strong-

ly one of the fundamental tenets of the Organization of African Unity, which is that African problems should be solved by African countries and not by outside interference" (*Bulletin,* June 1978, 29).

The administration demanded that the Cubans and Soviets withdraw from the region as soon as the Ethiopian-Somalian conflict ended. It consistently presented the Soviet-led intervention as a threat to peace in that part of the world and called for a peaceful resolution of the Eritrean-Ethiopian conflict. During his visit to the United Kingdom, April 13-23, 1978, Secretary Vance warned that "it is clear to us that if the Eritrean issue is determined through the use of force by foreign troops, bloodshed and suffering will increase, no enduring solution will be found, and tensions in the region will only be heightened" (*Bulletin,* June 1978, 25). When he returned from his trip to Moscow and London, Vance reiterated his position on this issue in an interview on the CBS television program "Face the Nation." Vance then added: "This is a problem that should be solved by the Eritreans and the Ethiopians" (*Bulletin,* June 1978, 30).

A few weeks later, President Carter also said, "Let us see efforts to resolve peacefully the disputes in Eritrea and in Angola. Let us all work not to divide and to seek domination in Africa but to help those nations to fulfill their great potential." In another press conference, one week later, Carter warned about an impending Soviet-led Ethiopian offensive in Eritrea. "We now have the prospect of a further armed outbreak between Eritrea and Ethiopia. And I would hope that our expressions of concern would induce the Cubans not to become involved in that fighting itself... I think it is time for the Cuban troops to withdraw from Ethiopia" (*Bulletin,* August 1978, 6-7). Slowly, the president's tone began to reflect that of the Brzezinski faction, which continued to advocate a more aggressive response to meet the Soviet-Cuban challenge in Africa. "The Soviet Union can choose either confrontation or cooperation. The United States is adequately prepared to meet either choice," he said (*Bulletin,* July 1978, 16).

Consistent with the American policy of removing all the factors that invite foreign intervention and lead to the further radicalization of the continent, the policy makers called for the withdrawal of the Somalis from the Ogaden, and the honoring of the colonial borders of the nations in the region. Also consistent with the American policy that African problems should be solved by Africans, Washington encouraged the Organization of African Unity (OAU) to intervene in the border dispute between Ethiopia and Somalia. Slowly, he came to realize that the OAU "has been relatively reluctant in the past to deal with very controversial issues. And quite often the African nations themselves are divided on the controversial issues" (*Bulletin,* August 1978, 7). Beyond that diplomatic move, however, the administration was not willing to do anything else to force the Soviet-led foreign forces out of the Horn of Africa. It rejected a proposal to link the Horn crisis to the SALT talks. Vance, along with the majority of the foreign policy team, rejected the linkage proposal: "We do not initiate any government policy that has a linkage between the Soviet involvement in the Ethiopia-Somalia dispute on the one hand and SALT or the comprehensive test ban negotiations on the other" (*Bulletin,* April 1978, 20).

WESTERN SAHARA/MOROCCO

Generally speaking, the Western Saharan issue was the most ignored of the three designated cases by both the policy makers and the press. The recurring theme in the American policy for this region during this period was United States relations with Morocco, a highly valued pro-Western nation. Communism was used as a reverse argument to justify more American arms transfer to Morocco.

Communism

Marxist ideology and Soviet intervention in Africa did not figure prominently in the Carter policy for this region—not to the extent we saw in the other two territories in this study. However, it appeared in several ways, one of which was Morocco's strong stand against communist expansion in the continent. One of the key reasons American policy makers cited to justify arms transfers to Morocco "to defend itself from Polisario attacks" was King Hassan's continued opposition to the Soviet and Cuban intervention in the continent (*Bulletin,* October 1979, 53). The State Department also tried to portray the conflict as if it was between Morocco and Algeria, a left-leaning African nation that some people placed at the time in the Soviet bloc. Algeria was and still is the staunchest supporter of the West Saharan struggle.

Moderate Nation

The United States and Morocco have had close relations at both the regional and global levels. The Carter administration viewed Morocco as a close friend:

- Because of its moderate position on the conflict between Israel and the Arab nations and the Palestinian people;
- Because "it has the largest Jewish population of any country in the Arab world—almost 20,000—and encourages the return to Morocco of Jews who have migrated to Israel,"
- Because the King of Morocco was the first Arab leader to support Anwar Sadat's historic visit to Israel;
- Morocco consistently supported moderate forces in Africa. Twice it sent troops in response to requests from Zaire to maintain stability in that country's Shaba Province.
- It also opposed Soviet and Cuban intervention in Africa (*Bulletin,* October 1979, 53).

- The State Department repeatedly accused the Polisario of attacking part of Morocco proper in the southern part of the country, a charge used to justify Washington's continued transfer of arms to Rabat. "The Polisario's decision to increase the scope and intensity of the fighting has made the quest for peace more difficult. It has also made it more difficult for us to maintain Moroccan understanding for a United States arms supply policy of great restraint" (*Bulletin,* October 1979, 54).

Though there was an escalation of the armed struggle of the Western Saharan people, the United States tried to put the dispute as one between Morocco and Algeria, instead of Morocco and the Saharan people and their universally recognized representative, Polisario. The United States, which recognized Morocco's administrative control of the territory, "continued to believe that the question of its ultimate sovereignty remained unresolved" (*Bulletin,* October 1979, 54).

Initially, the armed conflict forced Washington to "continue [its] historic role of arms supplier to the Moroccan government but only for weapons to be used to defend the territory of Moroccan proper." But, the Department of State admitted that "this policy has been easier to enunciate than to implement, and at times it has become a sticking point in our bilateral relations with Morocco." Washington was perceived as being so pro-Morocco on this issue that it neither attempted to mediate nor seriously push Rabat to resolve it peacefully. "We have not ourselves offered to mediate because of the number of other countries and organizations which are already involved and which are better placed than we to perform this service" (*Bulletin,* October 1979, 54).

Following the 1979 OAU conference held in Liberia July 17-21, William C. Harrop, Deputy Assistant Secretary for African Affairs, reported to the Subcommittee on African Affairs of the House Committee on Foreign Affairs that the "summit adopted the so-called Wisemen Report on the Western Sahara and asked the five states composing the ad hoc committee (Nigeria, Mali, Ivory Coast, Tanzania and Guinea) plus Liberia continue its work" (*Bulletin,* October 1979, 43). The report called for a referendum in Western Sahara as a vehicle for the people to determine their destiny. Harrop gave this report without indicating where the United States stood on these issues but added that it would be difficult to hold such a referendum without the cooperation of Morocco, which had walked out of the meeting in protest of the resolution. Walking out with it were Senegal and Gabon.

A few months later, the State Department sent Warren Christopher, Deputy Secretary of State, to Morocco to discuss Rabat's military requests. Discussing the visit, Vance repeated the charge that Morocco was being attacked not only in Western Sahara but also inside its own borders which, he said, forced the policy makers "to give more weapons to the Moroccans in order to give them the necessary strength to defend their own country and to put them in a position where they can negotiate a solution to the problem of the Western Sahara. I think that it is clear that none of us believe that there is a military solution in this problem. But clearly Morocco must have the weapons which it needs to defend itself" (*Bulletin,* December 1979, 26). The policy makers said, "It is difficult at this point to see how either side can win a military victory, but a peaceful solution to this dispute does not appear at hand" (*Bulletin,* October 1979, 54).

THE SECOND PERIOD (1981-1984)

As the Carter policy was in many ways a continuation of what Henry Kissinger put in place in 1976 for the Ford administration, the Reagan Africa policy picked up the militaristic tendency President Carter had exhibited during his last year in office, mostly in response to the Soviet invasion of Afghanistan and the widespread feeling that the Soviet intervention in Angola and the Horn of Africa was due to his unwillingness to use American military muscle. What was viewed as Carter's primary source of failure in the foreign policy arena—not being willing to use military force as an instrument of foreign policy during most of his presidency—was the main strength of Ronald Reagan's policy abroad. During this period, Reagan increased defense spending 40 percent and he and his conservative supporters were ready, able and willing to use force to fight the feeling of defeat and national paralysis that followed America's painful Vietnam experience. There is no question that Reagan's strong anti-communist stance greatly affected United States policy toward South Africa and the rest of the continent as we can see from the stated goals of the policy.

Among the key objectives of the Reagan administration's African policy were the following:

- To promote peace and national security and the denial of opportunities to adversaries;
- To support "proven friends" and be accepted as reliable friends;
- To support negotiated settlements in southern Africa;
- To help those nations that have development policies that work and are committed to democracy;
- To "do our part in meeting Africa's humanitarian needs and in fostering basic human liberties in keeping with both our principles and our interests (*Bulletin,* August 1981, 57).

In his first comprehensive statement on the new United States policy toward Africa, Chester A. Crocker, Assistant Secretary for African Affairs, speaking before the African-American Institute Conference in Wichita, Kansas, on June 20, 1981, listed the principles that governed the policy: "consistency in the pursuit of United States interests, reliability as a force for peace and stability, and balance in our approach to individual issues and the orchestration of policy." He also said that "as a nation we can no longer afford a foreign policy that confuses the American public because it lacks coherence, that confounds our allies because it lacks consistency, or that comforts our adversaries through its vacillations or ineptitude" (*Bulletin,* August 1981, 57).

The new policy had some major implications for Africa. It was designed to oppose and engage those on the left and work with those on the right believed to be America's friends in the fight against communism. Based on his strong anti-communist stance, Reagan characterized the Soviet Union as "an evil empire" and a source of all the regional conflicts in the world at that time. As a result, in the new administration's strategy, apartheid was viewed as a lesser evil compared to the communist threat to the region, United States interest and world peace. Secretary of State Alexander Haig said, " Years of sterile diatribe led South Africa to distance itself from U.N. Resolution 435 and to oppose a U.N. presence and involvement in the settlement process.... Our objective has been to achieve results rather than to engage in arguments" (*Bulletin,* January 1982, 17).

The new approach also undermined Carter's human rights policy since the target shifted to communism as the only focal point of the Republican administration's policy. Making it more costly for the Soviet Union to maintain its foothold in the Horn of Africa, as indeed in the rest of the continent, was also part of the plan, though there is little evidence to show that the administration was willing to back that up with money or weapons in the Horn. On the Western Saharan conflict, however, there seemed to be very little difference between the goals and approaches of the two administrations. This was the period during which the Reagan administration was trying to neutralize those African countries that were aligning themselves with the Soviet Union and to support pro-Western nations.

But, the most important difference between the foreign policies of the two administrations was, however, Reagan's well publicized support of pro-Western "freedom fighters." This support was enshrined in what is known as the Reagan Doctrine and the president said such a support was self-defense. "We must not break faith with those who are risking their lives—on every continent, from Afghanistan to Nicaragua—to defy Soviet-supported aggression and secure rights which have been ours from birth.... Support for freedom fighters is self-defense" (*Weekly Compilation of Presidential Documents*, February 11, 1985, 145). Although the targets of the Doctrine were outside of the territories designated for this study, one of them, Angola, had direct implications in the anti-apartheid struggle in South Africa. (The other targets were Afghanistan, Nicaragua and Cambodia.) Because of Pretonia's role in the anti-communist struggle and its support of the "freedom fighters" in Angola, the Reagan administration moved to ease the pressure the previous administration had put on South Africa to change its racist policy and advocated a policy they described as "constructive engagement."

"The time has come for us as a nation to erase any shadow of doubt about the importance of Africa to United States interests and to demonstrate by our actions that we can conduct a serious and sustained diplomacy in Africa," said the Reagan administration's chief architect of its African policy, Chester A. Crocker, in one of his major addresses on regional strategy for southern Africa. The administration also tried to strengthen United States ties with pro-Western nations. Previous American administrations attempted to do that but Ronald Reagan made no bones about working with right-wing dictators as long as that served American interests. Going into the last year of Reagan's first term, Crocker said that the administration had succeeded in creating an atmosphere "which permits useful discussion of those issues on which the United States and Africa must focus: security, economic development, tensions and change in southern Africa, humanitarian crises, and the strengthening of democratic institutions" (*Bulletin,* January 1984, 38).

The actual application of the Reagan policy in the three designated African territories will be examined along the same lines as that of the administration preceding it.

SOUTH AFRICA

There is no question that southern Africa was an issue that "occupied an important place on this administration's agenda—an issue of common interest to the Western world, an issue central to international stability," said Lawrence S. Eagleburger, Under Secretary for Political Affairs, in an address before the National Conference of Editorial Writers. "In retrospect, Western indifference to change in southern Africa played a part in creating" the crisis in the region. "As a nation we were not well equipped to deal with the region. Our involvement had been superficial; we knew little of its actors or its dynamics." Furthermore, Eagleburger told the editorial writers that the administration's southern Africa policy steered clear of the views of both the left and right wings. "Our body politic was polarized. The left was transfixed by the issue of racism, while the right was too often prepared to interpret events only in the light of the East-West competition." He then went on to criticize those on the "left" for advocating such measures as disinvestment (*Bulletin,* August 1983, 9).

The new administration's South African policy was based on three basic realities as perceived by the Reagan foreign policy team:

- The main American economic interests in Sub-Sahara Africa concentrates in and around South Africa;
- South Africa "is an increasingly contested arena in global politics.... It is [therefore] imperative that we play our proper role in fostering the region's security and countering the expansion of Soviet influence";
- Southern Africa is a highly complex arena, which must be understood on its own regional merits if we are to succeed in our efforts...Only if we engage constructively in southern AFrica as a whole can we play our proper role in the search for negotiated solutions, peaceful changes and expanding economic programs (*Bulletin,* February 1891, 25-26; emphasis mine).

80

The change also affected United States policy on the Namibian issue. Though the new administration continued to support U.N. Resolution 435, which called for Namibian independence, it decided to "elaborate the framework" of the resolution by "including certain constitutional guarantees...for the rights of minorities" and also establishing "an empirical relationship between the ultimate independence of Namibia and the continuing Soviet and Cuban presence in Angola." Secretary Haig, at a St. Louis town hall forum, said, "Although we intend to proceed unilaterally along the line toward Namibian independence, we cannot ignore this empirical relationship" (*Bulletin,* July 1981, 14).

Majority Rule

Though the achievement of majority rule in South Africa remained the stated primary goal of United States policy for that African country, there seemed to be less effort exerted to achieve it during the Reagan administration. But, members of the foreign policy team worked hard to dispel any doubt about the new administration's intentions regarding apartheid. Secretary of State George Schultz, for example, in remarks marking the 20th anniversary of the Organization of African Unity on May 25, 1983, said, "In connection with southern Africa and in connection with the apartheid system, I would say unambiguously, unequivocally, with no qualifications whatever, that the system of apartheid is unjust and unacceptable" (*Bulletin,* August 1983, 16; emphasis mine).

As the new administration began to explain and implement its African policy, it became clear that some of the original goals of the policy, including avoiding a race war and eradicating apartheid, were either modified or lowered on the priority scale on which "communism" and all its subsets—the Soviet Union, Cuban troops, radicalization, etc.—ranked the highest. Crocker, explaining the modified policy to the members of the Subcommittee on Africa of the House Foreign Affairs, said: "We seek constructive engagement with all the states of the region which wish the same with us.... The United States is on the side of peaceful change and negotiated solutions. This is where our interests lie, and this is what makes us uniquely relevant to the region" (*Bulletin,* April 1983, 50).

Human Rights

The new president slowly de-emphasized human rights, one of the pillars of the preceding administration's African policy. "Where we have an alliance with a country that, as I say, does not meet all of our [requirements]...we're in a better position remaining friends...than to suddenly, as we have done in some places, pull the rug out from under them and then let a completely totalitarian takeover that denies what human rights the people had." In fact, Reagan's choice as head of the human rights section of the Department of State was Ernest Lefever who, in a statement before a House Subcommittee two years before his appointment, said, "In my view, the United States should remove from the statute books all clauses that establish a human rights standard or condition that must be met by another sovereign nation" (*Bulletin,* April 1981, 11).

As a logical next step to their attitude toward Carter's human rights campaign, Reagan and his team began to deescalate the human rights campaign that had been directed at South Africa. "Can we abandon a country that has stood beside us in every war we've ever fought, a country that strategically is essential to the free world?.... I just feel that, myself, that here, if we're going to sit down at a table and negotiate with the Russians, surely we can keep the door open and continue to negotiate with a friendly nation like South Africa." However, though a concerted effort was made to play down human rights, the issue of race remained as important, if not more important than during the previous years, because the interests and demands of white South Africans seemed to have been given higher consideration by the Reagan administration.

The new human rights official was also quoted as having said that "we should not be concerned with South Africa's racial policies but should make the country a full-fledged partner of the United States in the struggle against communist expansion" (*Bulletin,* April 1981, 11).

Economic Sanctions

In line with its policy of 'constructive engagement,' the Reagan administration was strongly opposed to economic sanctions against South Africa. The policy of constructive engagement was carefully crafted to fight all efforts directed at severing the economic links between the West and South Africa. Eagleburger, then undersecretary of state for political affairs, told a group of American editorial writers in 1983 "it is essential that we in the West…send an unambiguous message to the people of [South Africa]. The message is, first that we agree with those South Africans who recognize that change is imperative, and second, that we are determined to permit them the opportunity to shape and define that change *free from the threat of foreign intervention*" (*Bulletin,* August 1983, 12; emphasis mine).

Developing Moderate Leadership

The administration was relatively successful in its effort to cultivate good bonds with moderate leaders of sub-Sahara Africa, though it did not seem to have made as much effort to develop moderate leadership in that region as the Carter administration had done. During the first two years, many African leaders were invited to the United States all of whom had something to say about apartheid. But, the documents show that Reagan and his African policy team could not sell "constructive engagement" as an approach to solving apartheid. President Kenneth Kaunda, who visited between March 29-April 2, 1983, expressed that they had differences especially on the Namibian issue. President Felix Houphouet-Boigny of the Ivory Coast, who visited between June 6 and 20, 1983, said that both leaders agreed on the need to fight "the enemies of freedom who find, in poverty and ignorance, the best fuel for their sinister designs." He added that "since prevention is better than cure, one must also be certain not to allow the perpetuation of unjust situations that foster them," a reference clearly directed at South Africa's racist system of apartheid.

There was also a similar American effort in other regions. To counter the regrouping of radical pro-Soviet nations in the north and eastern regions of Africa, the United States increased its security assistance to the moderate nations of Sudan, Somalia and Kenya as well as the Organization of African Unity (OAU) (*Bulletin,* January 1984, 38).

Communism (Soviet-Cuban Intervention)

Communism and all the other issues related to it—Cuban intervention, radicalization of the continent and even terrorism—took center stage as the primary shaper of United States foreign policy toward Africa during this period. Though this has been true of United States foreign policy since 1945, it was used as almost the sole determinant factor by the Reagan administration. Secretary Alexander Haig, in a National Foreign Policy Conference for United States Editors and Broadcasters at the Department of State on June 2, 1981, said, "I think we do believe that recent Soviet activity internationally is probably the greatest threat to world peace that exists today, either directly or in exploiting historic tensions that exist today in this period of transition" (*Bulletin,* June 1981, 21).

The administration attributed most of the political problems to the Soviets and their surrogates. President Reagan himself, in an address before the American Legion in Seattle on August 23, 1981, said, "The record shows that since the Soviets began their aid program in Africa in 1954, military aid has outpaced all other Soviet aid by seven to one. Then add more than 40,000 Soviet and surrogate military personnel stationed in Africa, and it's no wonder that Africa is rife with conflict and tension" (*Bulletin,* October 1983, 29).

As Reagan's first term in office approached the midpoint, it became clear that the issue of "destabilization" in southern Africa began to look like the centerpiece of the administration's policy toward Africa. Apartheid was viewed only as one aspect of this broad subject. In a statement before the Subcommittee on Africa of the House Foreign Affairs Committee on February 15, 1983, Crocker said, "My point is a simple one: The Cuban troop issue is not an issue we made up; it is an objective reality at the core of the question of regional security." In response to queries from the members of the subcommittee as to when the Cuban troop issue was linked as precondition for Namibian independence, the assistant secretary added: "Security, of which the Cuban troop issue is an integral part, has always been a prerequisite for agreement on Namibian independence. As a practical diplomatic matter, it will not be possible to obtain a Namibian independence agreement without satisfactory regional security assurances" (*Bulletin,* April 1983, 52; emphasis mine).

In another statement before the same committee a month later, Crocker explained, "Perhaps nowhere in Africa have our own security concerns, and our own security policies, coincided with African security needs and been more intensely engaged than in southern Africa.... It is also a region threatened with the prospect of heightened violence and polarization that could lead to great power confrontation. It is precisely to avoid that possibility of violence and confrontation that we have fashioned a major effort to bring about regional peace and security. We have launched a policy of constructive engagement with all the states of the region that wish the same with us" (*Bulletin,* May 1983, 22). More specifically, the administration sought "detente between South Africa and the other states in the region" (*Bulletin,* May 1983, 26). This was designed to help the administration implement its policy that was in place to prevent the destabilization of the region and, of course, to reverse the process of isolating Pretoria that had taken place as a result of the Carter administration's constant criticism of the racist system it practiced.

Crocker, in his assessment of the Reagan policy towards the end of the first term, was still optimistic. "This Administration, unlike some prior ones, has a strategy for achieving its goals in southern Africa, a strategy we call constructive engagement" (*Bulletin,* January 1984, 38).

ERITREA/ETHIOPIA

The key issues in the American policy for the Horn of Africa during this period were Soviet/Cuban intervention in the region, human rights and humanitarian aid. The previous administration tried to maintain good relations with Ethiopia, the most populous nation in the Horn of Africa, but at this point, the policy makers had come to the conclusion that was not going to happen with Mengistu Hailemariam in power. References to Eritrea are scattered throughout the documents but only in connection with humanitarian aid, refugees and the need for a peaceful resolution of the conflict. The key question of the Eritrean struggle, the people's right to self-determination, was not directly addressed in any of the documents of this period or the period preceding it, though there was an occasional reference to Ethiopia's territorial integrity, a stand used to signify American opposition to Somalia's claims in the Ogaden as well as Eritrea's demand for independence.

Communism (Soviet-Cuban Intervention)

The policy for this region was to counter and, if possible, reverse the growing Soviet influence in the area and address the fundamental conditions that the Soviet Union and its proxies—Cuba, East Germany and many other East European nations—tried to exploit in the Horn of Africa as well as the rest of the continent. The Soviet Union was viewed as the biggest threat to peace in this southern flank of the Middle East. Crocker, in a major foreign policy address before the American Legion in Honolulu on August 29, 1981, expressed the Reagan administration's concern about the influence in Africa of the Soviet Union and its satellites. He stated that "the United States has no desire nor, for that matter, any mandate to act as the policeman of Africa. But let there be no misunderstanding: This country will not hesitate to play its proper role both in fostering the well-being of friends in Africa and in resisting the efforts of those whose goals are the opposite. Without a minimum of regional political order, our other regional interests—humanitarian, economic, commercial—cannot be pursued" (*Bulletin,* October 1981, 24).

American and Western concerns about Soviet actions and intentions were heightened even more when the pro-Soviet radical nations in the region, Libya, Ethiopia and the People's Democratic Republic of Yemen, signed a 'tripartite pact.' The State Department said that "the new entente between Libya, Ethiopia, and South Yemen—three of the Soviets' closest friends in the area—is only the most recent of many threats to the security of our friends in the region" (*Bulletin,* October 1981, 13). As part of its effort to resist external aggression and prevent further destabilization of the Horn and the surrounding areas, Washington increased security assistance to pro-Western countries, like Sudan, Kenya and Somalia, as well as organizations, like the Organization of African Unity (*Bulletin,* January 1984, 38).

The policy also tried to show that violence was not the way to solve the many problems that plagued the region. In his assessment of the Reagan policy achievement going into the last year of the first term, Crocker said, "We have made clear our readiness to assist in any way we can in the resolution of longstanding tensions in the region, especially in the Horn of Africa, which have been the cause of so much war and suffering in the past" (*Bulletin,* January 1984, 39). However, the policy makers recognized "that peaceful progress in the developing world will become impossible if we fail to impose effective restraints on the use of force by Cuba, Libya and other Soviet proxies," said Haig, in a testimony before the Senate Foreign Relations Committee (*Bulletin,* October 1981, 13)

Human Rights

Washington repeatedly denounced the Ethiopian regime for its violations of human rights in both Eritrea and Ethiopia. Uni ted States Ambassador to the United Nations Jeane L. Kirkpatrick, in a statement before the U.N. General Assembly on October 2, 1981, responding to remarks made by the Ethiopian Minister of Foreign Affairs accusing the United States "of stifling progressive movements, undermining sovereign states," said that it was "his own regime [Ethiopia] that is engaged in a war against its own ethnic minorities [sic]—among them the Eritreans, the Somalis, and the Tigrayans." The United States representative said that the unfounded accusation was designed principally "to shift the blame onto others for their own internal failures and external acts of aggression" (*Bulletin,* February 1982, 81). The United States Department of State repeatedly accused the Ethiopian regime of gross human rights violations.

Humanitarian Aid

In response to media pressure to increase humanitarian aid even to nations that were under communist influence like Ethiopia, Crocker strongly defended the Reagan policy: "The United States is a major source of long-term and emergency food to Africa. We have an unparalleled record of assistance in addressing this problem.... The long-term problems of food production and availability are also being urgently addressed." To address the problem of refugees, the United States had made substantial contributions to programs designed to help the displaced in neighboring countries, he said (*Bulletin,* January 1984, 38). However, as we will see below, the press argued that the United States could have done more to save starving Ethiopians and Eritreans.

WESTERN SAHARA/MOROCCO

Reagan's policy toward this region had one overriding goal: To strengthen United States-Moroccan relations. Even America's occasional attention to the Western Saharan conflict was to meet that basic goal. United States policy makers showed more interest and began to be more active on this issue after several developments within the OAU and the United Nations. As a result, it seemed that Morocco would be isolated and the Polisario would gain in its diplomatic and political struggle for recognition and support of the Western Saharan people's demand for self-determination. First of all, the OAU added some teeth to its resolution and it became clear that if Morocco refused to enter into a serious negotiation on both the ceasefire and referendum aspects of the decision that Polisario would be made a member of the organization. Furthermore, the U.N. General Assembly's Fourth Committee adopted a resolution supported by Algeria, which was easily accepted, denouncing Morocco as an occupying power in Western Sahara and recognizing Polisario as the legitimate representative of the people of Western Sahara. As a compromise, Morocco supported the lesser of the two evils: the OAU resolution.

United States policy makers were forced to take sides. The State Department said the United Nations resolution "prejudged the issue and to some degree contradicted the Wisemen recommendation for a referendum which would allow the inhabitants of Western Sahara to express their own preference.... We do not embrace any particular solution to the conflict, although the OAU call for a ceasefire and a referendum does appear to us as a useful basis upon which to move forward" (*Bulletin,* February 1981, 55). This was how the official foreign policy organ summarized the action: "The Assembly adopted an Algerian resolution, on which the United States abstained, calling for negotiations to settle the future of the people of Western Sahara but prejudging the outcome by declaring that they should lead to the creation of an independent Saharan state and referring to the Polisario ...as "representative of the people of Western Sahara." The United States, in its statement to the committee, explained that it was neutral on the eventual status of the territory which can be decided only after due consultation with the people of the territory. It voted for a Moroccan resolution in which Morocco pledged to cooperate with the Organization for African Unity in settling the issue (*Bulletin,* June 1981, 55-56).

Washington continued to provide Morocco with arms and other support "to defend its territory." The Polisario issue was also a factor that United States policy makers repeatedly cited to justify their support of the Morocco regime (*Bulletin,* October 1981, 28).

Chapter 4

WHAT THE RECORDS SHOW:
THE EDITORIALS

The First Period (1977-1980)

During 1977-1980, the *Washington Post* and the *New York Times* carried a total of 87 editorials on the three selected territories dealing with practically all the issues seen in the official foreign policy documents from the *Department of State Bulletin*. Also, during the same period, the two newspapers carried 20 editorials categorized in their respective indices under Africa, dealing with issues affecting the continent as a whole. However, because these 20 editorials were not directly related to the three movements/territories, on which this book focuses, I have only used them for background discussion purposes.

Out of the 87 editorials from 1977 to 1980 dealing with the three territories or liberation movements, 47 were from the *New York Times* (See Table 1 and Figures 2 and 3). However, as is seen later, this numerical relationship reversed during the second period when the *Washington Post* carried by far the large majority of the editorials dealing with the three territories (See Table 3 and Figures 3 and 4).

However, one issue consistent in both newspapers was the emphasis given to South Africa, which represented by far the majority of the editorials during both the first and second periods of this study. As Table 2 shows, nearly 82 percent of all the editorials during the first period dealt with issues relating to apartheid, South Africa and those affected by them in the region. Those dealing with Eritrea/Ethiopia constituted about 15 percent, while editorials on Western Sahara represented only 3 percent of the total during this period. And, as shown in Figure 5 in the next chapter, Western Sahara was neglected even more during the second period. All the editorials on Western Sahara were from the *New York Times*. The *Washington Post* index does not have a single editorial entry on the issue during both periods.

Table 1. Editorial spread during the study period

Newspapers	1977	1978	1979	1980	1981	1982	1983	1984	Total
Washington Post	23	14	3	0	2	3	9	25	79
New York Times	26	15	5	1	6	5	7	6	71

Table 2. Editorial attention given to the three movements and territories

Territories	1977	1978	1979	1980	1981	1982	1983	1984	Total
Eritrea/Ethiopia	5	8	0	0	0	0	2	6	21
ANC/South Africa	44	19	7	1	8	8	14	25	126
W. Sahara/Morocco	0	2	1	0	0	0	0	0	3
Yearly Total	49	29	8	1	8	8	16	31	150

Table 3 A comparison of the two periods

Territories	The Washington Post		The New York Times		Total
	1st Period	2nd Period	1st Period	2nd Period	
Eritrea/Ethiopia	7	7	6	1	21
ANC/S. Africa	33	32	38	23	126
W. Sahara/Morocco	0	0	3	0	3
Total	40	39	47	24	150

Attempts will be made in Chapter Five to explain why the Western Saharan crisis did not get much editorial attention in these papers though the main national liberation front in the territory was recognized by the Organization of African Unity as the legitimate representative of the Saharawi people.

The key themes in these editorials were basically the same as those addressed in the documents reviewed in the previous chapter. These were communism, democracy/majority rule, sanctions, moderate leadership, human rights, and humanitarian aid. The issues of armed struggle and national liberation movements were addressed, most of the time, indirectly and through all the efforts the two administrations exerted to find "moderate African leaders" to undermine the political acceptability of the guerrilla leaderships in the different territories.

SOUTH AFRICA

As stated above, South Africa was in the center of editorial attention during this period. Four out of five editorials dealt with the problems of southern Africa, which gravitated around South Africa and its apartheid policy. Almost all of the problems that American policy makers focused on in this region had racial dimensions. Although most of the editorial pieces on South Africa put the spotlight on apartheid and communism, the other themes we saw in the previous section were also given some attention.

Majority Rule

There was a general agreement on the abhorrence of apartheid, but there was a constant debate on tactics and strategy in dealing with it. Up until July 1977, five months after Jimmy Carter took office, *Washington Post* editors kept the pressure on the administration to formulate an Africa policy but cautioned it to proceed on apartheid "at a pace appropriate to the complexity and volatility of the problem." However, the newspaper said that at least on apartheid laws "governing choices of sex and marriage…the necessity to confront them is painful but clear" (July 12, 1977, A18).

The *New York Times* accepted the general thrust of the administration's policy, though there were differences on tactics, on pace and method. When policy makers decided to drop "black majority rule" as their desired goal in South Africa and replace it with just "majority rule," the paper accepted the change but was "saddened to note that the semanticists in Washington are riding higher than the policy makers" and urged the administration to "concentrate on turning up the pressure toward realizable ends" (April 5, 1977, 32).

The *New York Times* also supported the general direction of the policy which advocated the "dismantling of at least those aspects of the apartheid system in South Africa that require forced migration and that deny blacks their citizenship" as "condemnation of such gross violations of human rights might be effective because of the chilling effect such criticism could have on American investment in South Africa." The editors, in their first assessment of Carter's African policy, said, the new administration "has begun to show that it grasps both the urgency and the subtleties of the situation in southern Africa" (May 17, 1977, 32). Reiterating their position a few months later, the editors said, "Until South Africa's suppressed blacks are granted basic political rights and liberties, outsiders are certainly justified in pressing for a system that conforms to democratic concepts" (September 23, 1977, 24). Both newspapers kept reminding Pretoria that failure to change the system could adversely affect not only the interests of South Africa but also those of the United States. The *New York Times* put it this way: "We may argue together about the pace of change, but not about the direction. *We shall suffer together if we fail*" (October 23, 1977, 16E; emphasis mine).

Both papers applauded the South African regime for every step it took to 'reform' the system. For example, the *New York Times* came out with an editorial supporting Prime Minister P.W. Botha regime's action in September 1979 to allow black labor unions to "have a right to negotiate and to strike under the same general rules as whites. At the same time, they will be subject to closer government supervision and risk losing their new status should they become too militant for the authorities' taste. In short, they have been given a privilege, not a right" (September 27, 1979, A18). By mid 1979, the *Washington Post*, after presenting both sides in the argument on whether apartheid has the capacity to reform itself, said, "Almost no one, however, can pretend to have anticipated the full scope of reforms, plans and stated official intentions that have come to light in South Africa in recent days" in the different areas of the public sector as well as in the regime's attempt to consult the nonwhites in matters that affected their lives (May 27, 1979, C6).

However, in a critical editorial on the South African court's decision to exonerate the police officers accused of beating Steven Biko to death, the *New York Times* said, "Such a conclusion shakes any remaining hope that blacks can receive justice from white South African courts" (December 3, 1977, 22). In fact, by the beginning of 1979, the South African regime had begun to scuttle some of the key agreements it had reached with the United States and the rest of the major Western powers on reforms. In early April of that year, without any warning, it expelled.... American military attaches for "spying." The *Washington Post* saw it as "South Africa's apparent readiness to back away from a foreign policy of conciliation" (April 15, 1979, 14A). Two weeks later, the newspaper said it was more convinced that the "spy"

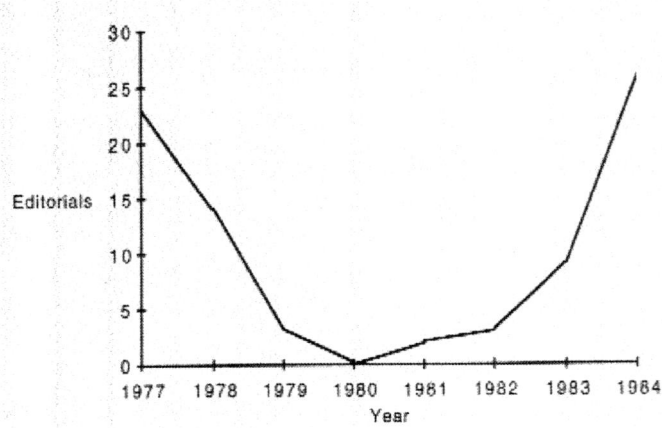

Figure 1. Number of *Washington Post* editorials, 1977-1984.

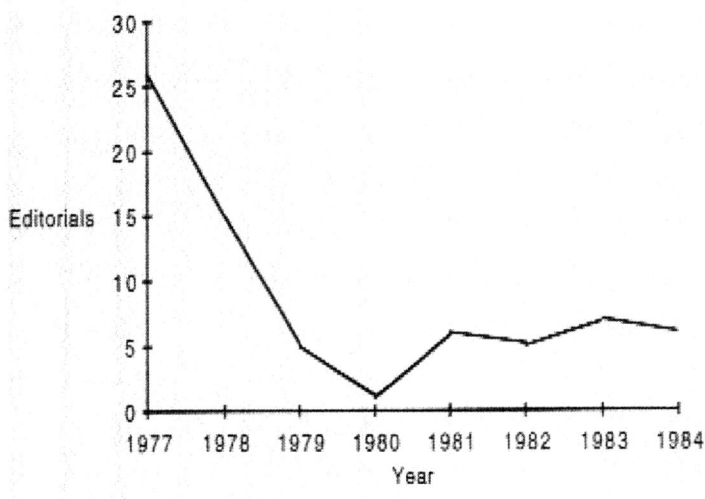

Figure 2. Number of *New York Times* editorials, 1977-1984.

charges were a smokescreen to hide the real intention behind the South African action. The editors of the Washington paper still supported the Carter policy for South Africa, but added, the United States policy has "not adequately gained the parties' confidence, perhaps least of all South Africa's. The United States is losing the capacity to influence events," and suggested moving up a meeting date scheduled between the American president and the South African Prime Minister (*Washington Post*, May 2, 1979).

Economic Sanctions

Both the press and the policy makers advocated putting pressure on Pretoria, but were opposed to economic sanctions. The *Washington Post*'s position was clear right from the start: "We don't like sanctions. This has nothing to do with favoring apartheid. It has to do with the conviction that sanctions are a poor and possibly self-defeating tool to use against a system so powerfully entrenched.... To start down the sanctions road is not what a responsible government ought to do just to satisfy its outrage or to keep up with the international Joneses.... The beginning of wisdom here is an awareness of the United States' own limitations" (October 26, 1977, A14). However, it is important to note that three days later, the *Washington Post* backed the administration on arms embargo on South Africa. "Since arms are a means and symbols of repression, it is right that President Carter should react to South Africa's latest fit of repression by supporting mandatory United Nations sanctions against the sale of arms to Pretoria." But the newspaper added quickly that before any further actions are taken beyond arms embargo, the Carter administration "should discuss them publicly before they are decided in order to ensure the public support necessary to make the decisions work" (October 29, 1977, A14).

The *New York Times*, in an editorial criticizing a United Nations resolution imposing minimal sanctions mostly of a military nature, lauded the Carter administration for the additional unilateral measures it took to discourage new investments by United States companies and not allow South Africa to purchase items that could be used by police to control riots. "It will be measures like these, more than the arms embargo, that may begin to affect thinking among white South Africans. They depend upon investments from abroad to maintain their high standard of living while absorbing a rapidly rising population into the labor force" (November 5, 1977, L20).

During the second year of the Carter presidency, the *Washington Post* continued its opposition to economic sanctions, although it hailed a congressional measure that prohibited the Export-Import Bank from providing financing to exporters to South Africa. "We are not enamored of the idea of economic sanctions against South Africa. They are a blunt weapon, pressing on both whites responsible for repression and whites seeking reform, on blacks who welcome that pressure as a move against apartheid and on blacks who see it as an invitation to harsher racial confrontation and to hardship for blacks as well as whites." The newspaper also was not sure "why South Africa alone should be singled out for its internal defects" (May 5, 1978, A18).

Both newspapers also applauded the steps the South African government appeared to have taken in support of reform in the economic field. The main steps taken were: a) official recognition of black trade unions, b) promise that black workers would be paid equal for equal work, and c) "some barriers against blacks' attendance at public events were lifted." However, in its assessment of the issue near the end of the Carter presidency, the *New York Times* said, "The rights of the black trade unions have actually been restricted; several union organizers have been detained, the unions cannot raise money abroad and there is a threat to prevent fund-raising at home as well" (June 20, 1980, A30).

Practically all the policy documents reviewed above make it very clear how important South Africa was to the American and Western economy. So, right from the start, the Carter administration's strategy was to make sure that this important economic link between the two countries was not fundamentally and adversely affected. The key policy strategy was to move between two extreme positions: one which advocated maximum use of American diplomatic, political as well as economic muscle to dismantle the racist system, and the other, which advocated that apartheid be relegated to the back burner in favor of focus on communism. Some of the measures taken were designed to give the appearance of action against apartheid to prod Pretoria to move toward change, but without pushing the whites into a corner. For example, Washington reiterated its widely publicized position against an arms embargo, which had been in effect since 1962, while resisting calls for "disinvestment" throughout the four years of the Carter presidency.

Communism (Soviet-Cuban Intervention)

The feeling of abhorrence the press exhibited against apartheid on the editorial pages was not based solely on moral grounds. Like the policy makers, the press believed in removing all factors that nurtured, attracted or were used as pretext, by the communists to intervene in Africa. The elite press, like the policy makers, felt apartheid was one of these factors. The scenario that the press repeated was that if the whites in southern Africa failed to move rapidly toward majority rule or accept meaningful concessions, the communists would move in and do it for them. For example, the *Washington Post*, in an editorial criticizing South Africa for balking at accepting a Namibia plan worked out by Western powers, said, "The sequence is foreseeable if Pretoria runs its own elections: The SWAPO will resume guerrilla war and invite the Cubans, with all that means to the American effort to provide a peaceful non-communist option for the settlement of African disputes" (September 22, 1978, A16).

The press also used the same argument to influence domestic American opposition to the Carter policy for South

Africa. In an effort to convince conservatives within the foreign policy establishment, in and outside of government, on the few sanctions the administration had agreed to, the *New York Times* said opposing the Carter policy would only result in the Soviets and Cubans calling the shots in southern Africa. The conservatives opposed Carter's sanctions on grounds that "that hampers the [South African] regime's fight against guerrillas and to give up the effort to win more power for blacks." The newspaper also said, "In embracing the whites of southern Africa in the name of opposing terrorists and Reds, the West would only guarantee the guerrillas' dependence on Russians and Cubans—and alienate the African nations that are trying to win true black rule by political means" (May 15, 1979, E36). The clamor to develop moderate black leadership was also another effort to preempt Soviet and Cuban designs for the continent by finding an alternative to the guerrilla leaderships of the different liberation movements which were widely viewed by American policy makers as being either communist or communist influenced.

Human Rights

Both newspapers welcomed the human rights component of the policy and its implementation right from the start, especially in the territories where communism was viewed as a direct and immediate threat. Less than two months after the Carter administration took office, the *Washington Post* said, "Jimmy Carter's arrival at the White House has newly sensitized the entire international community to the human rights question. He has made it clear that United States will move its own policy closest to those nations that share its values" (March 14, 1977, A22).

In its first editorial on the issue after Jimmy Carter took office, the *New York Times* expressed support of the administration's decision to reduce American aid to some pro-Western nations "where serious and widespread violations of human rights have been well documented." However, the newspaper "interject[ed] a note of skepticism," not an objection, when Secretary of State Vance told a Congressional subcommittee "that the administration was not prepared to take similar actions against the governments of countries where we have overriding strategic interests, such as South Korea or the Philippines" (February 27, 1977, 16). The editors noted that "apartheid in all its forms is first of all an issue of human rights" and, though the United States should recognize its limitations in bringing about fundamental changes in South Africa, that "is no reason—or excuse—for indifference to its stubborn march toward disaster" (October 27, 1977, A22).

Developing Moderate Leadership

Washington's effort to nurture and develop a black moderate leadership in South Africa was viewed as a logical step to Washington's mistrust of the leaderships of the national liberation movements. And policy makers had the full backing of the press on this issue. For example, the death of Steven Biko in police custody was viewed by both the policy makers and the press as a blow to this effort. Editorializing on the death of Biko, the *Washington Post* concluded: "In a broader context, those in South Africa who prevent blacks from developing their own leadership corps and who back off from meaningful dialogue with the black community, are sowing the wind. *Without the Steven Bikos, they will surely reap the whirlwind*" (September 15, 1977, A26; emphasis mine). In another editorial two months later, the *Washington Post* said, "The moderates knew well how tenuous their position was within the black townships. *They will now be virtually helpless to refute the contention of their sons and daughters that violence is the only sure path to change*" (October 21, 1977, A22; emphasis mine). As indicated above, the *New York Times* also came to the same conclusion. "Steven Biko was the kind of black leader—prepared to negotiate with whites, able to lead a substantial part of the black community—with whom any sensible white would have wanted to consult. Instead, he was murdered, and now his murder is covered up," said the *Washington Post*, in its denunciation of the court decision exonerating the South African police in the death of this young leader (December 4, 1977, C6). Denouncing the cover-up that preceded the court ruling, the *New York Times* strongly criticized the South African government for conducting the propaganda campaign it waged in an attempt to link Steven Biko and "the 'black consciousness' movement he founded with the revolutionary terrorism he specifically abjured" (October 11, 1977, 34). The paper said that Steven Biko's death "deprives South Africa of yet another *moderate and responsible voice for evolutionary change*" (September 15, 1977, A26; emphasis mine).

The editors of the *New York Times* also saw the arrest of Winnie Mandela in early 1977 as a blow to the efforts being made to develop voices of true African leadership. "Without such voices, there is no chance at all for peaceful reform" (May 23, 1977, 24). It must be noted that Winnie Mandela, who then headed the Soweto Black Parents Association, was not viewed at this point as a revolutionary leader.

The newspapers and the policy makers agreed that the South African crackdown in October 1977 and similar actions before and after in which many "moderate" leaders were jailed, their organizations banned, black-owned newspapers shut down and the homes of many prominent black leaders and white supporters raided, only defeated the purpose. In an editorial aptly titled "Courting Disaster in South Africa," the *New York Times* said, "The South African government seems determined to create precisely those conditions that will transform its largely moderate black opposition into an extremist and violent force" (October 29, 1977, A22). A week later, the newspaper said, "the important thing now is to give notice to South Africa of the world's dismay at its suppression of moderate black leadership" (November 5, 1977, L20). In yet another editorial, three weeks later, the paper predicted that "new black leaders will replace those jailed or banned, and their followers will grow

more militant as they observe the failure of the moderates"
(December 2, 1977, A26). The depth and strength of the
press's support of the human rights component of the
African policy continued through the rest of the Carter presidency.

ERITREA/ETHIOPIA

Despite its recognition that the Eritrean struggle "was different from the tribally-based secession movements common in other parts of Africa," the *New York Times* continually refused to recognize the Eritrean people's right to self-
determination. In fact, both newspapers continually labeled
it "secessionist" and never even seriously considered the
political issue behind the armed struggle. The Eritrean issue
was discussed only as part of the larger East-West conflict
and the *New York Times* raised the legitimacy of the movement and concluded that it was not a "tribally-based secessionist movement"(April 22, 1978, 18L) to make its case
why the Cubans should not intervene in Eritrea as they had
done in the Ogaden.

Though the Eritrean armed struggle started more than a
decade and half before Jimmy Carter came to the White
House, the press did not have to face the thorny question of
the Red Sea territory's self-determination until this time.
During this period, the movement showed enough military
muscle to attract world attention. In fact, by 1978, the liberation forces controlled over 85 percent of the Red Sea territory. So, in addition to the issues of communist intervention,
human rights and humanitarian aid, both policy makers and
the press had to address the issue of the territory's right to
self-determination—and they both supported Ethiopia's
'territorial integrity.' Based on that and noting the fact that
the OAU was not sympathetic to the demands of the
Eritrean people, the press and the policy makers felt they
were justified in coming out against the aspiration of the
Eritrean people. One year after the policy went into effect,

the *Washington Post* concluded: "The United States has shown a dedication to the principle of territorial integrity—Africans outside the Horn should appreciate that. It has shown that it is prepared to try to work out African disputes on African terms.... The hope must be that American diplomacy is earning the United States extra African support in coping with them" (11 March 1978, A18). In looking for a solution, they kept appealing to the Ethiopian regime to solve the problem peacefully, but never considered the leadership of the movement as a contributor to a solution.

Communism (Soviet-Cuban Intervention)

As indicated above, United States policy makers viewed the Soviet Union and its proxies as the main source of the problem in the Horn of Africa. On the Soviet-Cuban intervention, the press agreed with the administration's decision that ruled out United States intervention in the region. As an approach, the State Department favored what the *Washington Post* called a "diplomatic preemption" to deprive the communists of "the sort of aggrieved gunmen the Russians customarily hitch their wagon to" (February 2, 1978, A18). The papers fully endorsed this approach.

Both newspapers expressed great satisfaction that the communists seemed to have found a Vietnam-like quagmire in the Horn. In its first editorial on the Horn of Africa during the Carter presidency, "The Horn—and No Dilemma," the *New York Times* commended the administration for not getting directly involved. "The Russians are deeply enmeshed in the conflict, which makes it all the more remarkable, and commendable, that the United States is not.... The highest American interest, therefore, is to be sympathetic to both sides without involvement." The editors also have this warning to the Soviets: "The Russians have gambled their entire position in East Africa on a situation that is beyond their control. As an assertive international power, they have much to learn" (October 19, 1977, A24).

The *Post*, while advocating the same message of neutrality on the conflicts in general, felt that the Soviets might gain some acceptance by siding with Ethiopia in its war in Eritrea. The *Washington Post* believed that "for supporting Addis Ababa, which faces a serious secessionist challenge from its Red Sea province of Eritrea, the Soviets and Cubans will win respect from some Africans, suspicion from others" (April 25, 1977, A22). Nevertheless, the paper still felt that neutrality was the best political choice in the Horn.

The headlines of the editorials in both the *New York Times* and the *Washington Post* told the message: "Keeping Cool in Ethiopia" (February 3, 1978, A22); "Stepping Back from Ethiopia" (April 25, 1977, A22); "Stuck on the Horn," referring to the Soviets (January 13, 1978, 12); "Still A Quandary in the Horn" (March 11, 1978, A18). Like President Carter, the press strongly questioned the Soviets' staying power in the region. And like the policy makers, the press also believed in avoiding all pretexts for the Soviet Union to prolong their stay in Ethiopia. In fact, Eritrea, the victim of Soviet-Cuban aggression, was viewed as one of the reasons that necessitated, and even justified, the intervention. The *New York Times* said, "Without approving the colonel's [Mengistu] style of rule or choice of friends, Americans should recognize that any support for the invading Somalis or the secessionist Eritreans would be resented not only in Ethiopia but in most of Africa where territorial integrity is prized above all.... If the threat of disintegration were overcome, any Ethiopian government might move to reduce dependence on Moscow" (February 3, 1978, A22). *New York Times* editors added, "In the Horn of Africa, the deplorable intervention by any outside forces must be seen against the fact that it was precipitated by last summer's Somali invasion and seizure of the Ogaden region" (February 15, 1978, A24). In another editorial, three weeks later, the *New York Times* revisited the issue and said, "The Ethiopians may have been imprudent to depend so heavily on Soviet and Cuban aid, but they needed help and no other sources seemed remotely likely to provide it" (March 10, 1978, A28).

Ironically, the *New York Times* also saw Eritrea as a test for the Cubans to prove that they were not the tools they had become in the Ogaden conflict. *"The case of Eritrea is very different from the tribally-based secession movements common in other parts of Africa"* and questioned Havana's public statements favoring political rather than military solution to the conflict. "Why then has Havana sent additional troops to Ethiopia, even after Somalia's retreat from the Ogaden? Is a military solution being prepared? If [Castro] intends to keep Cuba out of the Eritrean quarrel, he has an opportunity to act accordingly" (April 22, 1978, 18L; emphasis mine).

Both newspapers agreed with the majority on the foreign policy team led by Secretary of State Vance on whether or not to link Soviet-Cuban intervention in Africa to the SALT talks. Taking advantage of the division within the team on this issue, the *Washington Post* suggested that Moscow should be put on notice that its continued meddling in the continent may lead to such a linkage. "We don't like the idea of holding SALT hostage to Ethiopia, but the Russians should know that, as a practical matter, this is the way things are likely to move unless they apply restraint. Washington may be stuck on the Horn. Moscow is, too" (*Washington Post*, January 13, 1978, 12). In another strong editorial, 'Son of Linkage,' two months later, clearly siding with the position of the State Department on the issue, and opposing arguments that had been put forth especially by Zbigniew Brzezinski, the Washington paper said, "To hitch SALT to Ethiopia is to burden SALT without helping in Ethiopia…. A good arms control agreement is far too important to the United States to be held hostage to the Ethiopian dispute" (March 3, 1978, A22).

Human Rights

The violation of human rights was another recurring theme in the policy. However, whenever the administration's strategy to contain and even reverse Soviet influence in the region collided with the principles of human rights, as in the case of Eritrea, there was a tendency to ignore the latter to achieve the former.

WESTERN SAHARA/MOROCCO

The two key factors that motivated United States policies for southern Africa and the Horn of Africa—namely race and communism—were not present in the Western Sahara conflict to the degree we saw in southern Africa and the Horn, and here the press seemed to have had a freer hand in taking a position on the controversial issues, even if that position was contrary to that of the United States government. But, at the same time, we also see the same neglect that characterized regions and crises that were not crucial to the immediate East-West issues of the time. Though there were more than 250 stories relating to the struggle in the two elite newspapers over the eight years of the study period, there was little editorial attention given to this conflict in these newspapers. In fact, the *Washington Post* Index does not have an editorial entry for Western Sahara for any of the eight years of the study period, though it carried a total of 37 stories referring to the conflict during the same period. The *New York Times* carried 214 stories during the same period, and editorialized on the issue three times, all during the first period of the study period. As a result, the editorial comments on the conflict or related issues are limited to the *New York Times*, which consistently advocated for the United States not to get involved in the conflict though it admitted that King Hassan of Morocco was a close friend of the West and a trusted American ally on Middle Eastern issues. "By any comparable calculation of interest, the United States should stay out of [King Hassan's] conflict," though he "is a valuable friend who often provides important support for American policies in the Middle East and Africa—when that support serves common interest." The editors also said, "After the Iranian debacle, the Carter administration has been looking for opportunities to show that it knows how to stand by old friends. The Sahara is the wrong place for such a demonstration" (October 16, 1979, A20). The *New York Times* editors reiterated that Morocco's security was not threatened, though the administration repeatedly claimed that the guerrilla group was conducting military operations inside Morocco proper.

Communism

The other reason behind the *New York Times'* strong opposition to United States involvement in the Western Saharan crisis had something to do with communism—or, more specifically, the absence of a visible communist threat in the conflict. The editors did not see any tangible sign of Eastern bloc interference to warrant American diplomatic quid pro quo. "There is no clear evidence of direct Soviet assistance to the Polisario guerrillas," said the paper and advised the policy makers that "instead of encouraging King Hassan to crawl further out on a military limb, the United States should join others in promoting a face-saving compromise. That will be difficult enough. Abandoning American neutrality would make it impossible" (October 16, 1979, A20). The editors also consistently noted that Morocco's claim to the former Spanish colony was not internationally recognized.

The Second Period (1981-84)

During the second half of the study period, there were 67 editorials in the two newspapers, 23 percent less than in the previous four years, on the designated territories (See Table 3). Of these, more than 89 percent was on South Africa and the rest on the Horn of Africa. As indicated in the previous section, during this period there was no editorial item entry recorded in the respective indices of the two newspapers on the Western Saharan conflict. This time around, the *Washington Post* carried more editorials on the territories than the *New York Times*. The Washington paper ran 43 editorials (64 percent) as compared to 24 listed in the *New York Times* Index and analyzed for this study.

Because of the conservative nature of the new Republican administration and as a result of statements made by Ronald Reagan during the 1980 presidential elections, some changes in the goals, approaches and implementation of the United States policy toward South Africa and the Horn were expected. But, the *New York Times*, in its first editorial on the issue of African policy in relation to the Reagan administration, said, "White South Africans may mistakenly expect a fundamental shift in American policy." The paper also warned "that the same mistake was made in 1979 by white Rhodesians, who felt relieved of the pressure on them once the right-wing Mrs. Thatcher became Britain's Prime Minister."

"In truth, no clear and fundamental shift is inevitable in Washington. The American style in Africa may change, and policy priorities may be juggled, but under President Reagan, no less than under President Carter, the United States is likely to keep its political distance from South Africa, and to keep pressing it for liberalizing changes....As much as the Carter liberals, the incoming Reagan conservatives will have to cope with an abiding reality. The future of Africa does not lie in the corner into which the Pretoria regime has painted itself" (*New York Times*, December 16, 1980, A22).

SOUTH AFRICA

As soon as Reagan took office, his administration began to send out trial balloons signaling that it was going to make some major changes in United States foreign policy. Three months after the *New York Times* predicted that the United

States would "keep its distance from South Africa" and two months into the Reagan presidency, the editors of that paper were disturbed by the new president's attitude toward the racist regime in Pretoria. In an editorial entitled "Drifting into an African Policy," the paper questioned some of the televised views of the president, which tended to see South Africa as a strategic partnership and concluded that "such a partnership would open the way to even deeper penetration of Africa by the Soviet Union and its Cuban helpers. This hard truth is taken for granted by the toughest-minded Europeans, including Britain's Margaret Thatcher" (March 22, 1981, 18E).

The same day, the *Washington Post* expressed its concerns about the new administration's African policy direction. Though publicly President Reagan had dismissed "strategic partnership" with South Africa, the paper said, "by a series of deeds, the administration has encouraged widespread fears in Africa and in the United States that it intends to do precisely what the president says he will not do—embrace South Africa, apartheid notwithstanding" (March 22, 1981, A22). Three weeks later, *Washington Post* editors also questioned Reagan's "optimism" in his views on how best the United States can contribute to the international effort to bring about change in South Africa. "The Reagan answer is not yet in full view, but in his statements the president has expressed more understanding for the white minority that is under pressure to yield power than for the non-white majority that bears the brunt of apartheid. He is, moreover, more optimistic than most about white readiness for change" (April 14, 1981, A18).

Majority Rule

The two newspapers seemed to have concluded right from the start the Reagan approach, which in effect wanted to relax the pressure against Pretoria, was unlikely to work. Both papers repeatedly said that, though P.W. Botha came to office in 1978 with warnings to his fellow white South Africans "to adapt or die," none of the steps he had taken was to disturb the power relations between the races. "And since the Reagan administration relaxed the pressure against apartheid and offered him 'constructive engagement,' Mr. Botha has become even cloudier" (*New York Times*, May 24, 1982, A18).

This issue was repeated in many of the rest of the editorials. The papers put to test the Reagan approach of constructive engagement as a means to bring about change in South Africa—instead of the Carter approach of keeping the heat on to force the racist regime to institute fundamental changes that would lead to a majority rule in that country. Three weeks later, the *New York Times* criticized Pretoria and its "foreign apologists" for intransigence to change the existing social power relations. "In no vital respect does Pretoria show a willingness to moderate the cruel laws that mark South Africa as a place apart. And incredibly, those laws may soon be made worse." The editors also criticized Washington for inaction. Though "some modest changes have occurred, and [Botha's] government proposes a limited extension of political rights to 2.5 million persons of mixed blood and 850,000 Asians... in theory and in fact, two-thirds of all South Africans remain foreigners in their own land. It is an inhumanity that American silence would compound if the pass laws become still more and more barbarous" (September 19, 1982, 18E).

The editors of both newspapers continued to feel that the Reagan administration was not doing all it could to pressure the white minority regime in South Africa. In response to a series of bombings in Pretoria, which killed 17 white and black South Africans and wounded 217 three years after the new conservative American policy of constructive engagement went into effect, the *New York Times* noted that Bishop Desmond Tutu "has tried consistently to touch the troubled conscience of his white overlords." The *New York Times* said additionally that, "President Reagan also has a chance, if he will but use it, to speak to that same conscience on behalf of all those in South Africa, white and black, who yearn for peaceful change instead of hatred, repression and death" (May 26, 1983, A26).

Assessing Ronald Reagan's image in relation to South African blacks at the end of his first term, the *Washington Post* said, "President Reagan has an unfortunate lack of evident empathy for the plight of South African blacks" (December 9, 1984, C6). The *New York Times* called the South African policy of giving Colored and Indians some voice while keeping blacks totally voteless "shamocracy in South Africa" (September 2, 1984, 14E).

The press continued to challenge the Reagan approach and attitude toward apartheid because the editors felt that was not the best way to fight communism in the continent. Both newspapers also pointed up the diplomatic cost Americans may have to pay in Africa for being friendly with pariah South Africa. Both administrations sought to have good relations with African nations while still working with the South African government. "Obviously, the [Reagan] administration—in this respect like the last— would like to have its cake and eat it too: to enjoy good relations, variously defined, with black Africa and with white South Africa" (The *Washington Post*, April 14, 1981, A18). Both believed in the carrot and stick approach—though Carter tended to be more stick ("keep the heat on" approach) while Reagan believed more carrot ("constructive engagement" approach) would work better. The *Washington Post* also strongly criticized the Reagan administration for allowing Pretoria to slip "past the international effort led by Jimmy Carter to grant independence to the colony it took over from the Kaiser's Germany after World War I" and for being "extremely solicitous in caring for Pretoria's security and political interests in Namibia." It concluded that "the very hint of American collusion to enable a regime Africans detest to harden its grip on a fellow African people undercuts American interests in the region" (September 6, 1981, A24).

The *Washington Post* also believed that, in addition to Namibia, the Reagan administration's favorable attitude toward UNITA and its leader, Jonas Savimbi, would adversely affect United States relations with the rest of Africa. " To support [Savimbi] is to fall into a partnership with South Africa that could cripple American dealings elsewhere in Africa, and it is also to give Luanda yet another pretext—Savimbi as well as SWAPO—to cling to the foreign communists whose presence most troubles the administration in the first instance."

Both papers concluded that constructive engagement failed on all fronts. On the diplomatic front, the policy was to lead to Namibian independence. But, Washington had nothing to show on the diplomacy side of the policy. "One early fruit of engagement was to have been the end of South Africa's illegal occupation of neighboring Namibia. The great prize of a regional bargain—independence for Namibia and the departure of Cuban troops from Angola—continues to elude Washington's grasp" (*New York Times*, November 18, 1984, 24E).

The *New York Times* concluded on the issue of race relations that the policy of constructive engagement may in fact have strengthened the system everyone was working to get rid of. The administration "thinks warm ties to that government" through constructive engagement "will achieve more good in the end. But it has nothing to show inside South Africa for four years of such engagement." It noted that trying to change such a fiercely defended racist system is difficult. "One can acknowledge the dilemmas of trying to alter that system by outside pressure. But 'constructive engagement' seems only to be reinforcing it" (November 18, 1984, 24E).

Communism

Both newspapers repeatedly opposed the Reagan approach especially in southern Africa because they both felt fighting communism while at the same time establishing partnership with the racist regime in South Africa was a losing game. The *New York Times* argued for a meaningful change in southern Africa and against the Reagan administration's friendly attitude toward the regime in that country in order not to create the conditions for the communists to penetrate the continent even deeper (March 22, 1981, 18E).

Continuing this warning in yet another editorial, the *New York Times* discussed "the risks of indulging South Africa" in great detail and warned against condoning South Africa's military attacks inside Angola. The Cuban and Soviet "stay won't be shortened by South Africa's provocative assault—nor by America's winking at it." Explaining further, the paper said, "Now Angola can claim, plausibly, that it sorely needs Soviet-bloc help to hold off the South Africans. And Moscow can pose, undeservedly, as the principled foe of colonialism and racism" (September 3, 1981, A18).

In an editorial in which the paper concluded that "the chief obstacle to the administration's effectiveness in southern Africa is itself," the *Washington Post* said: "The Reagan administration is bumping against the limits of its ideology in southern Africa. The true enemy, according to its latest policy pronouncements, is 'revolutionary violence' of the Marxist or Soviet-supported sort." The reference is widely understood to mean the revolutionary movements. "Yet to most Africans, and not only to them, 'revolutionary violence' is mainly the label that South Africa and supporters of its ways apply to those who challenge the power wielded inside and outside its borders by South Africa's white minority government" (September 6, 1981, A18). To some extent, the administration was successful in reducing potential cross-border violence directed at South Africa. The *Washington Post* said that the 1984 nonaggression pact signed between South Africa and Mozambique and a "dis-engagement" accord reached that year between South Africa and Angola represented a major transformation of southern Africa. The first agreement called on Mozambique not to allow the ANC launch operations out of Mozambique, and on Pretoria to withdraw its support of the anti-government insurgency in Mozambique. Pretoria wanted to use the second agreement to force Angola to end its support of SWAPO, then fighting to gain Namibian independence. The paper said, "There probably would have been no chance for this to take place without the diligent prompting of the Reagan adminis-tration. These events could yet constitute its single largest diplomatic achievement."

"For this sweeping transformation, however, South Africa's blacks may pay a cost. The ANC stands to lose much of its military capacity....It would be immoral to buy the diplomatic accomplishments, no matter how grand, at the expense of those long-suffering people," the paper said (March 13, 1984, A14).

Economic Sanctions

Both the *Washington Post* and the *New York Times* were consistent in their opposition to meaningful economic sanc-tions and disinvestment. The *Washington Post* justified its stance on the issue this way: "Although the economy under-girds the apparatus of white control, it is the engine of black progress at the same time. To disinvest is to slow that engine down." Citing a Ford Foundation study, and even noting the fact that the person who chaired that study was black, the paper said, "The weight of knowledgeable opin-ion, including black opinion, is plainly on the side of going slow on disinvestment" (March 10, 1983, A18). Both news-papers also seemed to have felt right from the start that con-structive engagement, as a strategy to end apartheid would not work. The Washington paper editorialized that "the phrase was meant to suggest the United States could get more change out of the white minority regime in Pretoria by a measure of political understanding than by the attitude of confrontation identified with Jimmy Carter.... [It is] a fancy name for showing some understanding of the political realities of the fellow you are trying to move." But, the paper added that "even in the Carter years, there was always a strong though quiet element of 'constructive engagement'" (October 18, 1983, A18). It strongly criticized a Congressional measure that prohibited "any new American investment in South Africa" and doubted if it was enforceable. "The trouble with unenforceable political gestures is that they divert effort from the kinds of slow and unspectacular work that might actually make a difference" (October 29, 1983, A18).

The *New York Times* said that it was understandable that Americans were "exacerbated by the Reagan administration's bland, unfruitful policy of 'constructive engagement' with South Africa. Even hard-boiled European traders now talk of adopting Sullivan-style restrictions on dealings there." However, *New York Times* editors did not think these voluntary fair employment restrictions for all American companies doing business in South Africa would work. They opposed an attempt made to legislate fair employment standards for United States companies in South Africa with more than 20 employees. The editors said, "Though a justifiable response to the inhumanity of South Africa's system, [legislating the standards] would be a sizable leap onto untested terrain and... the bill is probably the wrong way to press our values, and it may dismiss the voluntary program too readily" (June 15, 1983, A26).

The *Washington Post* supported the tactics of civil disobedience used by the Free South Africa Movement in the United States and the group's demand to end the Reagan policy of constructive engagement. "The Free South Africa Movement finds constructive engagement merely a disguise for American support and accommodation of apartheid.... Those Americans, however, speak for a central feature of the

American moral legacy. It is not wrong for them to demand that their government consider their imperatives. South Africans of all races should know that, while there is some division and confusion over tactics, a powerful American majority demands justice" (November 27, 1984, A18).

However, the *New York Times* backed a South African request for an I.M.F. loan, which drew widespread opposition. However, the newspaper said, "Approval with proper strings attached could help lift the shroud of South African injustice.... Denying the... loan outright would set a destructive precedent." The editors said letting "the [I.M.F.] raise the issue in negotiations over problems of the South African economy and acknowledge it in a few diplomatically worded observations attached to the loan... would make an important political point without undermining the fund's integrity" (October 20, 1982, A26).

Developing Moderate Leadership

The *New York Times* urged the Reagan administration to approve $5.7 million to train South Africans under a program developed by Harvard University. "In all South Africa in 1979, there were only 10 African engineers and 10 accountants, compared with several thousand whites. The same shaming disparity applies to medicine, dentistry, science and law.... Although the Reagan administration wants 'constructive engagement' with South Africa, it has yet to endorse this simple and appealing idea" (July 8, 1981, A26). The Reagan administration was viewed as being, at best, indifferent, at worst, on the side of the racist regime of South Africa on the question of protecting the black leadership inside protesting the system from within—but peacefully. For example, the *Washington Post* cited the case of six political fugitives who sought sanctuary in the British Embassy in Durban, South Africa, after leading a well-publicized boycott against a new constitutional system, which gave the Coloreds and Asians some political voice, but continued to keep blacks disenfranchised. The United States Embassy, when asked for assistance after three of these "moderate" leaders walked out of the British Embassy "to expose the South African government's disrespect for the rule of law," did not approve their request on the grounds their lives were not in any imminent physical danger. The United States response apparently was handed up "after Pretoria had declared that United States assistance to the fugitives would amount to encouraging a criminal act...[which] quite possibly conveyed a deadly impression of bowing to South African intimidation" (The *Washington Post*, October 8, 1984, A18). But, the editors did not want to argue with President Reagan for claiming credit for the release of 11 South African detainees a month later, on December 7, 1984. He said it was American "quiet diplomacy" that was responsible for the release of these detainees. "Mr. Reagan, having already made one statement on apartheid on Friday, popped up in public a second time to say that the release [of the political prisoners] was a fruit of his policy," the paper said, and went on to ask: "Now that you have confirmed the principle that American policy can be counted on to produce concrete results, what is to be your next success?" (December 9, 1984, C6). However, the controversy did not end there. In a third editorial in as many weeks, *Washington Post* editors said, whoever deserves the credit—the Reagan administration, the Free South African Movement, or the South African authorities—it was premature rejoicing because some of those released were rearrested and some more were jailed. "On the American side, however, there should be no premature rejoicing over gains that, on inspection, turn out to be wholly inadequate. Perseverance is what's indicated. Much, much more need doing" (December 18, 1984, F6).

In its denunciation of the crackdown that led the leaders of the United Democratic Front, a multiracial organization that fights to bring about change in South Africa through nonviolent means, to seek sanctuary, the *New York Times* also reminded the Reagan administration of the harsh realities of apartheid. It noted that President Reagan, in his congratulatory letter to Nobel laureate Bishop Desmond Tutu, said, "All Americans join me, in recognizing your labors in seeking to promote non-violent change away from apartheid, toward a form of government based on the consent of the governed and toward a society that offers equal rights and opportunities to all its citizens, without regard to race." However, "In South Africa, simply uttering those ideas can be a criminal act. And that is the disturbing reality the administration ignores in its passive response to the white regime's police-state crackdown on dissenters of all races, the worst in years. Those being arrested are not violent revolutionary conspirators but advocates of non-violent change, the disciples of Gandhi and Martin Luther King" (November 18, 1984, 24E).

ERITREA/ETHIOPIA

During the second period of the study period, the Eritrean movement went through probably the most trying phase in the history of the struggle. With massive Soviet-Cuban military, logistical as well as political help, the Ethiopian regime in 1982 mobilized all its forces and resources to "wipe out once and for all" the Eritrean struggle. This came in the wake of a brutal civil war between the Eritrean Liberation Front (ELF) and the Eritrean Peoples Liberation Front (EPLF), which led to the virtual disintegration of the former, the oldest of the two, as a fighting force inside the country. The Ethiopian campaign, known as Red Star, involved the largest human and material mobilization ever seen in the then 21-year history of the Eritrean-Ethiopian conflict. The Soviet-backed operation caused an unprecedented degree of human and material destruction, but it failed to achieve its goals and left the Eritreans stronger in terms of firepower. But, it was not given any editorial attention. The editorial themes in the press were communism and the famine that devastated the region in 1984-1985.

Humanitarian Aid

Regarding the drought and famine victims that had started to make the news worldwide, the *Washington Post* said, "In the wars going on in Eritrea and Tigray, food is a weapon of war. This is especially true of the Ethiopian regime, whose efforts to pry local populations out of their support for rebellion often seem to center on depriving them of food and the means of a normal existence, such as it is." The editors charged that "the United States has done relatively little to help Ethiopia meet its growing crisis.... This country [the U.S.] must help the starving Ethiopians and help them now" (June 27, 1983, A10).

The perception was that the Reagan administration was too preoccupied with fighting the "evil empire" to help starving famine victims in a Marxist-ruled nation. The famine was also at least partially attributed to the mismanagement of the economy and socialization programs by the ruling Marxist Derg of Ethiopia. The two papers, especially the *Washington Post*, urged the administration to set its ideological lenses aside and look only at the humanitarian aspect of this tragedy. The paper editorialized that the famine was the result of wrong policy choices by the Ethiopian regime and Soviet unwillingness to provide meaningful humanitarian and economic aid. "All that provides no reason, however, for the United States to fall away from its traditional position that relief of starvation knows no politics" (July 18, 1983, 12).

Then in 1984, in the height of one of the worst famine crises the Horn of Africa had ever seen, taking advantage of the election pressures that forces candidates to avoid controversial subjects, the *Post* editors wrote four editorial pieces on this issue still hammering the point that the United States could have done more. In its first of this series of editorials, the paper said, "A sharp little political dispute has broken out over whether the Reagan administration has moved smartly enough to meet the tremendous famine in

Ethiopia.... It is an unlikely subject for Americans to be arguing over in an election campaign, but the dispute will have been useful if it generates further help for those in need" (November 2, 1984, A22). The paper then strongly supported a "food truce" proposed by the leaderships of the Eritrean movement and another movement in the region, but rejected by the Ethiopian regime (November 23, 1984, A26). Three weeks later, the editors, in an editorial entitled 'Biting the Hand,' strongly approved the way American officials reacted to charges by the Ethiopian regime. "The United States was quite right to answer Ethiopia's charges that the countries trying to rescue Ethiopia from famine caused much of it. Rejecting the charges, United States AID Director M. Peter McPherson described them as a classic example of biting the hand that feeds you." However, the editors continued their push for more famine aid to the peoples of the region. "The Ethiopian government is scared and resentful, but the Ethiopian people are starving. It takes no time at all to decide to whom Americans owe their first obligation" (December 14, 1984, A23). And in the last editorial for the study period, which gave an overall view of the human tragedy in Africa based on a UNICEF report which revealed that those living in "absolute poverty" in Sub-Sahara Africa rose from 82% to 91% during the previous decade, the *Washington Post* made an even stronger pitch in support of its case: "Look at the numbers provided by UNICEF, watch the television pictures from Ethiopia, read of a 3-year-old who weighs 6 1/2 pounds, and ask if our approach to Africa does all it can to serve the continent's true needs" (December 31, 1984, A12).

Communism

Most of the references to communism or the Soviet Union in the editorials during this period were related to famine and drought in the Horn of Africa. The *Washington Post* editors repeatedly presented the human tragedy as a failure not only of the rulers of Ethiopia but also of the Soviet Union which guided the Derg along wrong policy choices which eventually led to famine and starvation. The papers also repeatedly blamed the communists for failing to respond to the tragedy as fast and as much as the situation demanded. So, the famine was viewed as a failure of the Marxist ideology that undergirded the policy that was said to have caused at least some aspect of the famine. The paper said, "the repressive Marxist regime now in power has cast its lot with the Soviet Union and its clients, Cuba and Libya. These friends of Ethiopia choose to leave it pretty much on its own when it comes to food" (June 27, 1983, A10). Three weeks later, the paper repeated the charges: "In Ethiopia, as elsewhere, Moscow continues to concentrate on furnishing arms, leaving it to the Western countries to pick up the requirements of relief, not to speak of development" (July 18, 1984, A12). The Washington paper severely and repeatedly criticized the Marxist regime in Addis Ababa for its misplaced priorities in both Eritrea and Ethiopia and continued to blame Moscow for the tragedy. "The Soviet Union has been the direct sponsor of the Ethiopian policies that aggravated the human and economic costs of the famine. Heat should be put on the Kremlin, which has behaved recklessly and cynically in this situation" (November 2, 1984, A22). In an editorial on the Falashas of Ethiopia, in which it advocated they be given "a decent exodus," the *New York Times* said at the root of the stagnation of the Ethiopian economy was the Marxist ideology of its rulers (March 2, 1984, A26).

However, at least in one editorial, the *Washington Post* editors praised the Eritrean Peoples Liberation Front for calling "a truce or negotiation to facilitate distribution of relief" (November 23, 1984, A26).

WESTERN SAHARA/MOROCCO

During the second period of this study, the annual indices of both daily newspapers do not have a single editorial entry on the Western Sahara-Morocco conflict. However, of the 214 stories relating to the conflict published in the *New York Times* during the entire period of this study, 96 or nearly 45 percent of the total appeared during the second period. Similarly, of the 37 Western Sahara related stories published in the *Washington Post* during the entire period, 14 or 38 percent were published during 1981-1984, though, unlike in the *Times* in which the articles were spread throughout the four years, all the *Post* stories appeared in 1981. However, these articles did not translate into editorial attention.

Chapter 5

THE PRESS AND THE STATE: A TWO-DIMENSIONAL INTERPLAY

A close examination and analysis of the data in the preceding chapter reaffirm the basic assumptions discussed in Chapters I and II, that there is a strong interplay between the elite press and foreign policy makers, and that the American press does not generally challenge the basic assumptions and goals of United States foreign policy. A content analysis reveals that this interaction has two sides, with one side showing an *interplay of support* for systemic preservation of the institutions of the press and the state, and the other side revealing an *interplay of influence* in the interest of institutional self-preservation, hence a tendency toward unity at one level in order to serve mutual interests and an instinct for competition at another for audience and legitimacy. The data also support the propositions stated in Chapter III that there is a relationship between the positions of the elite press and official United States policy stand on African liberation movements; and that generally, the American press does not seem to question the assumptions of United States foreign policy on national liberation movements in Africa. This can best be seen in the respective positions and views of the press and the state (as represented by its foreign policy makers) on the very nature of these movements, the internal and external factors that affect their existence as well as the issue of armed struggle itself.

Interplay of Influence

The interplay of influence between the press and policy makers is mostly characterized by each side trying to set the agenda for the other in order to take the policy initiative. As O'Heffernan says, "In the context of mass media and policy, 'agenda-setting' refers strictly to the salience of issues," involving the placement of a new issue or the elevation of it on the agenda (199, 45-46). As to who has the power to either introduce an issue that was not on the public agenda at the time or elevate the level of its salience, he quotes two key members of the Carter administration's foreign policy team as having two diametrically opposite views on the issue, a reflection of the diversity of perceptions of what the role of the press is in general and the nature of its relations with the state in particular. Furthermore, it also shows how policy makers perceive their own role in dealing with the press and how they interpret the interplay between the institutions of the press and the state.

This study shows that these two fast growing and powerful American institutions are locked in a constant struggle for audience and legitimacy in the eyes of the people as well as to influence each other's agenda. There is a general tendency on the part of the press to try to set the agenda whenever there is a policy vacuum, which may be due to a number of reasons including negligence on the part of the state. It may also be because it is too early in the life of a new administration. The press tends to try to fill the vacuum by lavishly offering advice or criticizing the administration for not having formulated a policy.

This contest for leadership as agenda setter during the period of this study became clear in the press's repeated attempt to take the policy initiative whenever there was a policy vacuum, most of the time evident during the early months in the life of both the Carter administration and the first term of the Reagan presidency. As will be seen later, at least on one issue, famine and humanitarian aid, the press, by elevating its level of public attention through sheer repetition and concentration, was also successful in taking the initiative which resulted in the policy makers speeding up the implementation of a policy strategy. This comes out clearly in some of the editorials from the early months in the Carter and Reagan administrations. Writing four months into the Carter presidency, the *Washington Post* asked, "What is Our African Policy?" In the absence of clear policy guidelines, the paper felt it necessary to demand that a policy be put in place as soon as possible, but also criticized some of the tactics of United States Ambassador to the United Nations Andrew Young's "undeclared psychological warfare" against apartheid and the white minority regime behind it. But, the issue was not Young's idiosyncratic style of conducting diplomacy, but "the Carter administration's failure to date to articulate or, as far as we know, to compose a coherent African policy" (May 8, 1977, C8). A month later, the *Washington Post* came out with its own "approaches to South Africa" in which it suggested that "at least transitionally, the Carter administration should be ready to recognize good-faith movement toward a political structure that falls short of the American ideal. Indeed, at this point, it would probably be tactically unwise to tell South Africans in advance how far and how fast they must go" (June 9, 1977, A18). Again, eleven days later, while admitting that a policy was indeed being developed at that point, *Washington Post* editorial writers hoped that answers to some key questions regarding tactics of how best to nudge the South African regime without pushing Pretoria to a defensive position "will emerge from a comprehensive statement of the administration's African policy, which is said to be in preparation." And it added this: "We hope [to see] a clear and cogent explanation of exactly what the President is up to in Africa, in general, and in South Africa, in particular, [which] is overdue" (June 20, 1977, A20).

The *New York Times* showed this interaction early in the life of a new administration in an even more direct way, in which one sees how the press and the policy makers go about defining and redefining the foreign policy issues before the official policy is formulated: "A friend in the [United States] State Department complains about a recent editorial which attributed to President Carter the view that he favors 'black majority rule' in Southern Africa. We were advised that the President and all official policy statements are being very careful these days to speak only of 'majority rule,' precisely because the United States wishes to avoid frightening Africa's white minorities and because 'majority rule' is a numerical rather than a racial idea that does not exclude whites from a ruling coalition."

The editors accepted the correction but they were "saddened to note that the semanticists in Washington are riding higher than the policy makers" and urged the policy makers to turn down the rhetoric and turn up "the pressure toward realizable ends" (April 5, 1977, 32).

Four years later, one witnesses a repeat of the same cycle during the first few months after Ronald Reagan began his presidency in January 1981. The *New York Times* editorialized on the new administration's "drifting into an African Policy," in which the newspaper urged the new foreign policy team to define and issue the Reagan African policy. "When will the administration calculate where it is headed in Africa? Does it really care?" The editors also went on to give their own views of the best tactics and approaches they thought Washington should follow to realize United States policy goals toward the continent in general and southern Africa in particular. The editors also reminded the policy makers to keep in mind through the policy making process that "Black Africans do not regard themselves as proxy pawns in Cold War chess" (March 22,

1981, 18E). The same day, the *Washington Post*, in an attempt to read into the new president's views in the absence of a clearly defined policy toward the continent, warned the administration against changing the policy goals that were set by Jimmy Carter and Gerald Ford, goals Reagan himself seemed to support in public: "By a series of deeds, the administration has encouraged widespread fears in Africa and in the United States that it intends to do precisely what the president says he will not do—embrace South Africa, apartheid notwithstanding" (March 22, 1981, A18).

Furthermore, whenever there was a division within the foreign policy establishment, the agenda-setters within the press went into full swing, influencing one side or another in the policy debate. For example, on the issue of linkage, when a division became apparent within the Carter administration foreign policy team, the press took a strong position against linkage, no doubt tilting the debate in favor of the Vance faction whose position became the official line during most of the Carter years in the White House. And when there was division between Congress and the administration on whether to stop the Export-Import Bank from financing loans to companies doing business in South Africa, the *New York Times* saw some merit in the administration's argument, but "greater merit in Congress going on record as willing to take concrete measures to express its abhorrence of Pretoria's racist policies" (April 25, 1978, 36).

On the other hand, the members of the foreign policy teams tried to set the agenda by using their privileged access to the press as the source of most foreign affairs news. The policy makers constantly tried to use the press to ensure domestic support for foreign policy initiatives, keep a policy momentum going or even influence events, groups, foreign governments and peoples. As Figures 3 and 4 show, the policy makers were successful in setting the topics for the press to editorialize on by determining what foreign policy issue or issues to stress at any given time. However, this may not be done in a conscious and deliberate way. The figures show a sharp decline in the number of editorials between 1977 and 1980, reflecting the Carter foreign policy team's preoccupation with non-African issues especially in 1979 and 1980, the most important ones being the Camp David Peace Accord, the invasion of Afghanistan and the Iran hostage crisis. The trend reverses during the second period of this study when the Reagan team came in vowing to deactivate Carter's "active diplomacy," trying to push issues like human rights, apartheid to the backburner, until 1984 when the media and the public forced the agenda on Reagan as a result of a series of daily and protracted public demonstrations in front of the South African Embassy in the nation's capital. The *Washington Post* attributed the role of agenda setting on this issue to the media and the United States-based Free South Africa Movement, which, through these well-organized demonstrations, is believed to have created a tremendous surge in public awareness in the United States about the racist system of South Africa. "The demonstrations have imparted a new intensity and interest to an issue that earlier was off most Americans' screen.... Do you think for one minute that President Reagan would otherwise have received Bishop Tutu, the South African Nobel Peace Prize winner? *Just a few weeks ago apartheid was simply not on the presidential agenda*, not something he had to devote his personal time to or prepare to talk about at a news conference" (December 9, 1984, C6; emphasis mine). In another editorial, a week later, the *Washington Post* said, "Mr. Reagan is being forced by the administration to demand more of Mr. Botha than he has in the past four years" (December 16, 1984, F6).

Almost all of the key issues the newspapers editorialized on—majority rule, human rights, constructive engagement, etc.—were initiated by the government. The first editorials were triggered by statements made by the new President and other government officials, especially

Secretary of State Cyrus Vance and his Assistant Secretary for African Affairs in the new Reagan administration, Chester Crocker. Though both papers expressed concern about the Reagan administration's initial attitude toward South Africa, the press was not challenging the policy already in place. In fact, the papers were advocating adherence to the Carter policy, which was still in effect during the early months of the Reagan presidency. At work, here was the policy makers' ability to pump up or down a story and the potential editorials that might come as a result of it. American politicians and bureaucrats are usually surrounded by public relations experts to manage the news for them. Brzezinski, one of Carter's top foreign policy advisors, said that the agenda setting function always rests with the White House, and insisted that "by and large we set the agenda" for the media (O'Heffernan 1991, 45).

In addition to the power to set the agenda, sources can also affect the level of editorial attention a subject gets in the press. A close analysis of the content of the editorials points to the commonality of sources and the role news sources play in affecting content. They also can create a semblance of uniformity of coverage and editorial subject matter. The literature review and this study reaffirm that the foreign policy officials serve as the main source of foreign affairs editorial subjects and, as a result, they have direct access to the press. There is no question that the Carter and Reagan foreign policy officials dictated most of what the press talked about and this power, in turn, resulted in the commonality of themes relating to Africa and the designated territories in this study. This also gave the officials the power to define the subject matter, focus on certain themes and draw the parameters of the discussion on any given subject, including those about national liberation movements, as will be shown below.

It is interesting to note that the attention level both the *New York Times* and the *Washington Post* gave or failed to give to the three territories runs parallel throughout the study period, except the last year when the number of *Washington Post* editorials showed a dramatic increase mostly due to the fact that in 1984 the Washington, D.C., based Free South Africa Movement, through well-organized actions of civil disobedience, turned the South African story into a local story. This, in turn, prompted more editorials in that Washington daily newspaper. The other subject that accounted for additional editorials in the *Washington Post* was the 1984-85 great famine, which ravaged both Ethiopia and Eritrea—a subject whose salience the *Washington Post* was successful in helping raise, though most of the credit was given to television. In its first editorial on the protests, the *Washington Post* stated, "It is not wrong for [the demonstrators] to demand that the government consider their imperatives. South Africans of all races should know that, while there is some division and confusion over tactics, powerful American majority demands justice" (November 27, 1984, A18). Two days later, in another editorial, the paper rejected arguments that had been made by the South African ambassador to the United States comparing the daily protests to the American Embassy takeover in Iran in 1979. Five days later, in yet another editorial on the protest, *Washington Post* editors argued in favor of a common moral standard for both black and white human rights violators in Africa so as not "to risk having the cutting moral edge of what they intend to be a lasting and growing political movement—something new in American politics—dulled right at the start" (December 4, 1984, A18). In the fourth editorial in about two weeks, the paper said that the consular protests were having an impact on the public and the government. And as was indicated above, forcing the president to talk about issues he had totally ignored, like apartheid, was "one measure of change" (December 9, 1984, C6).

Though most of the credit for elevating the level of significance of the famine story went to network television, more specifically the National Broadcasting Corporation

(NBC), there was no question that the elite press did have an impact on the policy makers. The overall impact of this process was believed to have increased famine funds almost tenfold. Congressman Bill Gray said, "When NBC showed pictures of the starving masses of Ethiopia [and Eritrea], America changed its foreign policy. People asked: Why are we not doing something about that? *The funds went up from $12 million to $107 million*" (Rosenfeld 1984, A27; emphasis mine).

What we see here is that the press, by emphasizing certain issues over time, increases public awareness of those issues, thereby leading the public and policy makers to perceive that these issues are more important than others are. Former United States ambassador to the U.N. Donald McHenry said, "In our system of government, issues frequently get attention only if someone presses the issues and the amount of attention depends on who presses and how

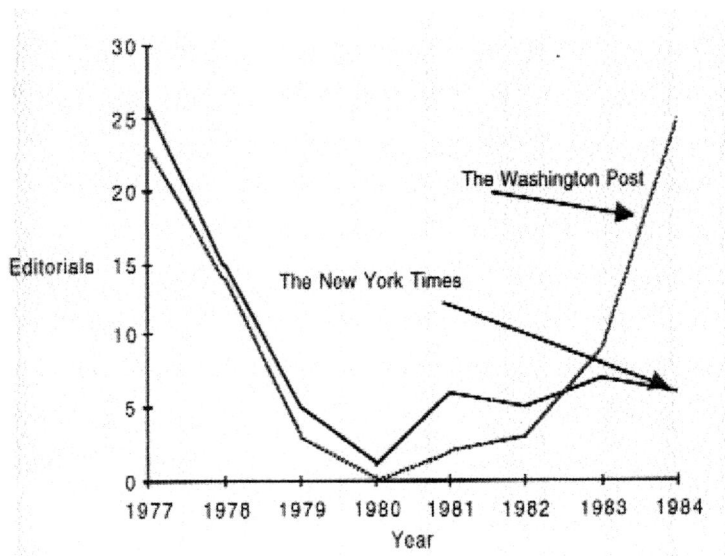

Figure 3. Comparison of *Washington Post* and *New York Times* editorial focus on the three selected territories.

strong" (1974, 148). It is believed that the policy makers perceive that the public is likely to believe that the issues stressed by the media are more important than others are. This can be viewed as another version of the two-step agenda-setting theory, which holds that the media influence their audiences who in turn force the policy makers to behave along certain lines.

The findings also show that when a story, because of its international magnitude or domestic impact, turns into a local or domestic story, as in the case of Vietnam after the Tet Offensive in 1968 when government officials lost most of the "power" they had to pump the story up or down at will, the domestic readership market comes into play. Despite its national and international impact, the *Washington Post* considers itself as essentially a local paper. The fact it is based in a city, which is over 77 percent black, is a crucial economic fact for the paper.

In addition to graphically depicting the sudden increase in the number of *Washington Post* editorials in 1984 during

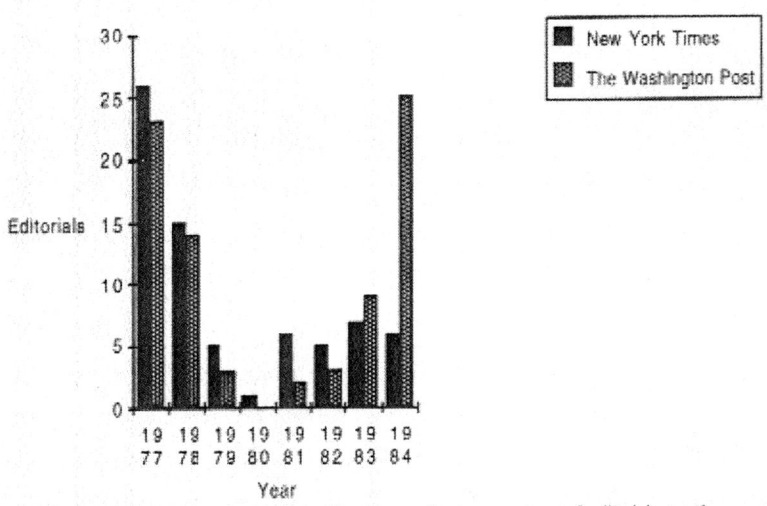

Figure 4. The *New York Times* and the *Washington Post* comparison of editorial attention

a period of highly-publicized and well-organized daily protests in Washington, D.C., Table 1 and Figures 3 and 4 show the overall spread of the editorials in the selected newspapers over the eight years and compare the attention level between the two newspapers during that period. Generally, the figures point to the two papers' tendency to reinforce each other's messages by focusing on practically the same subjects and giving relatively the same level of attention to these subjects. This seems to be more true when the press is dealing with foreign affairs news or related editorials which are few and far between.

Interplay of Support

There is also a strong interplay of support between the United States press and American foreign policy makers, a built-in function rooted in the system they both have an interest in preserving. In a way, this should not be surprising because the institutions of the press and the state, as discussed in previous sections, have a lot in common, despite the fact that the media try to portray themselves as mere democracy watchdogs and as disinterested transmitters of public information. The press, like the other institutional actors in the society, operates within "a shared cultural meaning," which serves as a frame of reference for journalists and policy makers (Arno and Dissanayake 1984, 1). "Although there may be references, even struggles, among the elite, among segments of the public (audience) and among the various kinds of media and the people who work in them, these conflicts would be transcended by the ideological frame of reference which forms the basis of social institutional integration" (Nwanko 1983, 3). John Adams wrote more than 200 years ago in the Massachusetts Constitution that a free press is crucial to the security of the state in a given society. Furthermore, though "the media do contest and raise questions about government policy, but they do so almost exclusively within the framework determined by the essentially shared interests of state-corporate power" (Chomsky 1989, 75). This is especially true in the foreign policy arena where the fierce competition one witnesses between media outlets in the domestic market is almost absent (Paletz and Entman 1981).

But, the interplay between the press and the state is even more evident during a period of crisis. The interaction between these two institutions intensifies when the state senses danger, especially of an international nature. O'Heffernan says he was not surprised that Bernard Cohen found in his 1962 study that "at that time the media worked closely with the foreign policy apparatus of the United States government and almost routinely supported American policy goals, not surprising given the Cold War and President Kennedy's skillful personal cultivation of reporters" (1991, XI). The Cold War represented an ongoing crisis throughout the post-World War II decades until 1988 when it was declared over as a result of the ushering in of a new era in United States-Soviet relations which had begun three years earlier when Gorbachev became president of the Soviet Union. "Since 1945, the United States has maintained a global foreign policy, American involvement worldwide has been based on a perception of a global struggle for power and influence with the Soviet Union, a desire for economic well-being through world trade, and a commitment to advancing principles of freedom" (Jordan and Taylor 1981, 133).

The period of this study represents the height of the Cold War in Africa with the Soviet Union projecting its power into the region to a degree and in a way never witnessed before in the continent. Prominent communist leaders made visits to several African countries. Ethiopia, the seat of the Organization of African Unity headquarters, had begun to move away from the West and into the socialist camp and Moscow began to effectively turn the turmoil in the Horn of Africa to its advantage. Soviet allies had taken over state power in Angola and visible signs of similar changes could be seen in what were to be Zimbabwe and Namibia. The intensification of guerrilla war in Zaire—one of the top pro-western nations in Africa—by Katanganese insurgents, was also seen as yet further evidence of Soviet intentions and influence in Africa. When Jimmy Carter took office in January 1977, Cuba had a presence in 16 African countries stretching from Algeria in the north to Mozambique in the south, from Ethiopia in the east to Guinea-Bissau in the west. The countries in between those geographical extremes with Cuban military and advisory personnel presence were Cape Verde, Guinea, Sierra Leone, Sao Tome and Principe, Congo, Angola, Madagascar, Equatorial Guinea, Uganda, Benin, Tanzania and Libya. Of these, Angola and Ethiopia had the majority of the Cuban military and civilian advisory surrogate personnel, with Angola having, according to United States sources, 19,000 troops and 300 medical advisors as of early 1977. The number of Cuban surrogate troops at the height of the Soviet-Cuban buildup in Ethiopia ranged from 17,000 to 20,000. Most of the Soviets in Ethiopia and Eritrea were given key roles in the planning and execution of the many large-scale military offensives the Ethiopian rulers launched in an effort to "wipe out" the struggle in that former Italian colony. At the end of the period covered by this study, the Soviets had more than 3,000 military "advisors" in Ethiopia, some of whom were captured in the decisive battle of Afabet in March 1988 which marked the beginning of the end of Ethiopian occupation of Eritrea. It must also be noted the Soviet Union built a naval base in the Eritrean archipelago of Dahlak on the Red Sea. In addition to its Eastern European satellites, the Soviet Union mobilized its "allies" in the region, mainly South Yemen and Libya, to an extent never experienced in the region before to ensure success of its foray into the continent. Though ironically Soviet weaponry was to play a crucial role in the defeat of the Ethiopian army 13 years later, it was this military hardware that sustained the Derg's war in Eritrea as well as inside

Ethiopia by equipping and constantly supplying a half-million-strong army in this poor and famine-ravaged country. Soviet expansion to the Horn was also viewed as a threat to American interests in the Middle East. Brzezinski described the Horn as "a region in close proximity to our most sensitive interests" (1983, 178). He recommended a strong show of force to send an unmistakable message to Moscow; however, the recommendation was rejected by the dominant faction within the Carter foreign policy team.

It was this unprecedented development that greatly concerned American policy makers and forced them to move in all directions to diplomatically preempt Soviet and Cuban efforts and influence. Namibia, for example, moved to center stage, as did Rhodesia (Zimbabwe), in United States policy in 1976. At a policy level, Washington had always supported the U.N. resolution calling for South Africa to relinquish its authority in South West Africa (Namibia), but as Vance put it, "until the Portuguese withdrawal from Angola and the subsequent growth of Soviet and Cuban influence, little was done to implement the [U.N.] decision" (1983, 272). Furthermore, as Bloom, Africa correspondent for the *Financial Times* of London, wrote in the *New York Times* at the time when the Carter administration was scrambling to put its African policy together in early 1977, "It is not the mere presence of the Russians and their allies—highly visible because of the visits of President Nikolai V. Podgorny and Prime Minister Fidel Castro of Cuba—but, also by supplying arms to victorious liberation movements, the Russians have put themselves on the side of the future" (Bloom 1977, IV-2). This future was seen in the growing success of the national liberation movements. In the eyes of Washington's policy makers, who never seemed to fully understand or accept the internal factors that lead to insurgency in developing countries, these movements were viewed as the Soviet Union's Trojan horses. Measured by any yardstick, therefore, this period indeed marked the height of the Cold War in Africa, and this was especially evident in the southern part of the continent as well as in the Horn.

But how did this affect the relationship between the press and the foreign policy makers? American national interest comes into play as a determinant factor in the press's decision-making process. In other words, during such times the press becomes less of a watchdog for democracy and more of a protector of the national American interest. In this study, this became evident in the views of the elite press and the officials on the key issues of a policy that was formulated to counter a serious threat to the national American interest in this part of the world. They agreed on: a) what constituted the "main threat" to peace; b) American interests in Africa; c) the goals of United States policy for the continent; and d) the national liberation movements. The documents and the editorials bring these out during both Democratic and Republican administrations despite sometimes glaring differences in policy approaches, style and rhetoric.

Both the press and the policy makers seemed to agree on the key goals of United States foreign policy for Africa. In addition to maintaining and strengthening the traditional economic links between southern Africa and the United States, two other major goals were put in place by Kissinger in 1976 after the United States was shaken out of its complacency in Africa when the Soviet Union began to project its power into the continent. These goals—to avoid a race war and containment of communism by preventing further radicalization of the continent—remained the key policy targets of the American policy makers during both administrations.

Race was high on the agenda of both the press and the policy makers. After the Soviets began to move into the continent in a massive way in the mid-1970s, then Secretary of State Henry Kissinger in 1976 moved left and right to blunt the communist intervention by raising the very issues Africa and Africans had been asking the West and especially the United States to support: the struggle against apartheid in South Africa, Zimbabwean independence and ending Pretoria's rule in Namibia. This high level United States attention to the continent was unprecedented. Traditionally, Africa had been ignored by both the policy makers and the press. In a frank admission of how the policy makers had practically ignored the continent, William E. Schaufele Jr., Assistant Secretary for African Affairs, in a speech before the American Academy of Political and Social Science at Philadelphia, said, "The African continent in general, and the southern part of it in particular, excited sustained attention and debate only among a small band of specialists in academia, business circles, and the government, except in time of crisis" (*Bulletin* May 1977, 464).

Up until 1976, the United States showed little interest in Africa. However, with the entry of the Soviet Union into the picture, starting with its major involvement in Angola using Cuban troops starting in 1975, United States policy for the continent took a new shift. The United States move also took another dimension: racial. The *Washington Post* in a 1976 editorial captured Washington's new attitude toward Africa well: "The United States, scared into a new concern for black liberation by the Soviet-Cuban intervention in Angola, will be asking [Prime Minister Vorster] whether South Africa will cooperate in an effort to bring majority rule promptly and reasonably peacefully to Rhodesia" (*Washington Post,* June 13, 1976, A18).

The interplay between the press and the government was therefore more evident on these two key determinants of United States policy for Africa at this time. However, though Carter's ambassador to the U.N. Andrew Young agreed that race might have been "the single most important dynamic in today's foreign relations," he felt that "Kissinger had no understanding of that and that was the reason he misjudged the situation in Africa" (Bloom 1977, IV-2). Of the two factors, communism seemed to have played the most defining role. This was even more so during the presidency of Ronald Reagan who portrayed himself as the primary fighter against the scourge that was Marxism-Leninism. However, both administrations were consistent in their public denials that neither communism nor race played a determinant role in the formulation or implementation of their respective policy strategies. But a careful reading of the documents reveal that some members of the foreign policy teams were a little more candid than what the official lines indicated. The Reagan team was also more open on the issue than its predecessor was. For example, Secretary of State Haig and his assistant secretary for Africa, Chester Crocker, were more direct in their views as to what extent ideology played in shaping their foreign policy. Crocker, for example, described the Cuban surrogate issue as "the core of the question of regional security" (*Bulletin* April 1983, 52). This was as much true in southern Africa as in the Horn. Inversely, it was also true in the Western Saharan case where both of these factors were absent or at such a low level that they did not affect the attention the movement was given by both the media and the policy makers.

However, though the policy goals remained basically the same, there were some serious differences within and between the liberal and conservative administrations in their approaches on how to achieve these targeted goals, and the press played its part as an actor in the foreign policy establishment. Jimmy Carter and his team wanted to put a great deal of heat on Pretoria to move toward majority rule so as to deprive the Soviets and Cubans of influence through the national liberation movements. This was part of an overall strategy that the Carter team had laid out to remove all conditions that either invite the communists to or help them perpetuate their presence in the continent. There were also differences within the Carter foreign policy team on the nature of the Soviet-Cuban threat and how to respond to it.

The Reagan team wanted to downplay the rhetoric against apartheid and move South Africa off the center stage to concentrate on communism Assistant Secretary Chester Crocker said that Washington did not intend to destabilize the regime in South Africa to win friends in the rest of the continent. The Reagan foreign policy team set out to tone down Carter's "activist diplomacy." To the conservatives in and outside of the foreign policy establishment, the Carter approach was perceived as being too much to the left and accused the administration of favoring a "communist-supported black guerrilla group," and Vance wrote that "some worked hard to compel us to support white-dominated solutions" in southern Africa (1983, 257). But, in the end, the Reagan policy makers adopted the very strategy they set out to change. Crocker, in his progress report of the policy going into the fourth year of the administration, said, "Ours is *an unprecedented activist diplomacy* in Africa aimed at addressing conflicts, strengthening genuine nonalignment, working for creative approaches to Africa's economic crisis, and creating options for peaceful change" (*Bulletin* January 1984, 38; emphasis mine).

When Reagan took office, the conservatives tried to implement their ideas and started off with a strategy designed to insulate Pretoria from the growing armed revolutionary movement which had bases in the surrounding countries. His policy of constructive engagement, for example, viewed the white racist regime in South Africa as a deserving and legitimate partner to work with. The nonaggression pact between South Africa and Mozambique and a 'disengagement' accord between South Africa and Angola, both of which were designed to curb the military capacity and reduce the operational theaters of the liberation movements in the region, especially the ANC, is a direct fruit of the policy approach the conservatives pursued.

But, despite the glaring differences between the two administrations in rhetoric and style, the policy goals remained the same. Chomsky, in his assessment of the

Reagan administration's Central American policy during the same period as in this study, says: "While [George] Shultz, [Elliot] Abrams, [Jean] Kirkpatrick and company occupy an extreme position on the political spectrum in their enthusiasm for terror and violence, *the general policy goals are conventional and deeply rooted in United States tradition, policy planning and institutions,* which is why they have received little attention or criticism within the mainstream" (1989, 103; emphasis mine).

Of the three territories in the study, South Africa had both policy ingredients—race and communism—and that was why it attracted the most attention from both the press and the policy makers as Figure 5 and Table 3 show. The primary reason behind the press's interest in the Eritrean-Ethiopian case was the same as that in South Africa: the threat of communism. Yet, the level of press attention to this region was much less compared to that given to South Africa; however, it was more than what the Western Sahara-

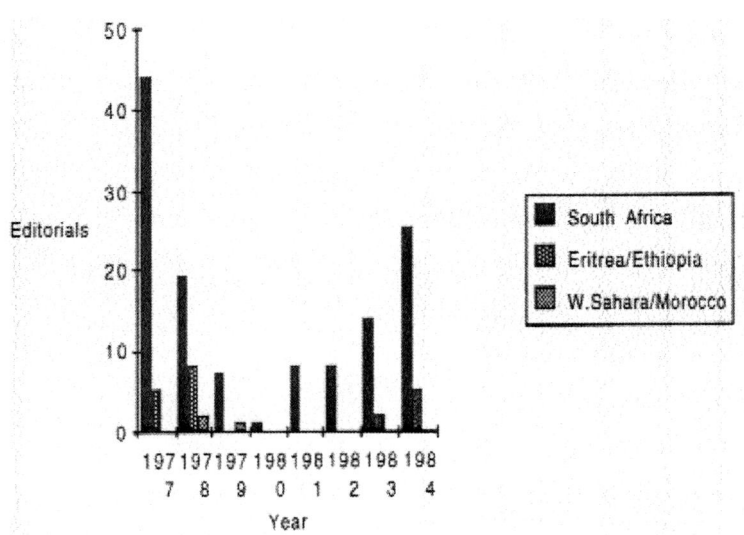

Figure 5. Comparison of editorial attention level of the three territories.

143

Moroccan conflict received, which attracted the least editorial attention during the period covered by this study. However, though the Eritrean struggle was fighting the Soviet Union and its satellites, Washington policy makers and the press were not willing to extend support to the movement because of other perceived American national interests.

When the two principles of human rights and territorial integrity clashed, as they often did on the Eritrean question, the policy makers and the press seemed to have found it to be more beneficial to the United States to go with the latter so as not to risk "losing" Ethiopia. The territorial integrity argument applied to both the Ethiopian-Somalia dispute as well as the Eritrean-Ethiopian conflict. In the case of the first, Washington meant the withdrawal of the Somalis out of the Ogaden territory, which they had occupied. In the case of the Eritrean-Ethiopian conflict, it meant accepting the Ethiopian argument that any support for the Eritrean cause would be violating Ethiopia's territorial integrity.

The same attitude was also at work in the Western Saharan conflict. The Saharan question was probably the easiest of the three cases in this study to understand and try to mediate since the annexation of the territory happened only two years before the new administration took office and the United States had not officially recognized Morocco's claim to that former Spanish colony. But, because it did not have the two key ingredients that shaped United States policy toward Africa during the study period, in a glaring way the case did not receive the attention given the two other African regions in this study. However, the support and sanction it was accorded by the Organization of African Unity kept the issue on the front burner and put United States policy makers "on the horns of a dilemma not of their making," said Harold H. Saunders, Assistant Secretary for Near Eastern and South Asian Affairs, in a statement before the Subcommittee on Africa of the House Committee on Foreign Affairs (*Bulletin* October 1979, 53).

Finally, the question that comes to mind is, if the basic goals of the two administrations were the same, why did the press constantly challenge and in most cases oppose the Reagan approach? At first glance, it may look like an in-house ideological clash between the liberal press and a conservative administration. Reagan constantly challenged the liberal tradition in American foreign policy, which the American press supported. There is no question that his foreign policy approach in Africa as in other parts of the world did challenge this tradition. The press also repeatedly criticized the conservative underpinning of his policy planning and approach. *Washington Post* editors felt that the chief obstacle to the Reagan administration's African policy was its own conservative ideology. But, that was not the main reason that the press challenged and sometimes opposed the Reagan approach. After all, there was very little disagreement on the main goals of the policy. The *New York Times* and the *Washington Post* did not believe his way was the best way to fight communism in Africa or prevent a race war in southern Africa. For example, the newspapers constantly expressed concern that Reagan's positive attitude toward the pariah state of South Africa would hurt United States interests and undermine American standing in the eyes of Africans and, as a result, would make it easier for the communists to spread their influence. The *New York Times* said, as a result of the new "partnership" Reagan established between Washington and Pretoria, "Soviet strength and credibility in Africa will be magnified. America's moral and political appeal would be vitiated" (3 September 1981, A18).

When Ronald Reagan took office, there was a consensus within the foreign policy establishment on the need for a majority rule in southern Africa to contain communism. Their support of majority rule in South Africa was politically motivated and was inevitably linked to the East-West conflict. Secretary of State Vance, Carter's chief foreign policy architect, wrote: "Like the previous administration after its conversion [in 1976], we recognized that identifying the United States with the cause of majority rule was the best way to prevent Soviet and Cuban exploitation of the racial conflicts of southern Africa" (Vance 1983, 257). Both the *New York Times* and the *Washington Post* had also concluded, as did the American policy makers, that the status quo in southern Africa, especially in South Africa, was no longer able to serve American interests and that apartheid put the interests of corporate America at risk. The newspapers said that apartheid actually was providing an opening to the communists. The data also reveal that the *New York Times* used the same argument to discourage conservative opposition to the Carter policy.

Attitude toward African Liberation Movements

Another key issue in this study that both the press and the policy makers seemed to agree on was national liberation movements. In fact, the main reason why Washington showed such a high level of interest in Africa during the study period had to do with these national liberation movements. United States diplomacy in Africa during this period was widely viewed as an effort to preempt the efforts of the movements and, as will be shown below, some of the policy makers and the editors were very open about it. Some of these movements, most of which started in the 1960s, had begun to come of age and showed that they had the military muscle to take state power. These armed and well-organized struggles for freedom represented the last and difficult stage in the decolonization process in Africa.

As was discussed in the preceding chapter, although the Reagan Doctrine injected a new element into the policy by supporting some "national liberation movements" in the world, including the South African struggle, the overall attitude of the policy makers and the press toward Africa's liberation forces in general remained unchanged. However, though these movements represented an important part of the two administrations' policies, and very much present in the editorials, references to them both in the documents and on the editorial pages were at best scattered, and at worst, covered up under tons of diplomatic niceties. In fact, the best revealing documents and editorials were those that tried to go around the issue without leaving any direct, open and clear references regarding these movements.

Nevertheless, the data clearly shows that, despite occasional disagreements on tactics and style, the journalists and officials seemed to have commonality of views on these movements throughout the study period:

1. They seemed to have the same perception of the nature and motivation of these movements.
2. Both sides misrepresented the political essence of these movements and the distortion emanated from the editors' and officials' common framework of what they perceived to be the reality in Africa.
3. Policy statements about social justice, human rights and human dignity, notwithstanding, their positions on the three movements were politically motivated.
4. Both were consistent in their opposition to armed struggle as a means to change the status quo.
5. Both tried to use the movements as a bogeyman to push United States policy goals especially in southern Africa.
6. Both seemed to agree on approaches that tried to marginalize and undermine the leaderships of these movements.

These national liberation movements were widely viewed as being too radical, probably communist and Soviet-inspired and bent on destroying Western interests. The documents and the elite newspapers show that the editors and policy makers failed to fully grasp the socioeconomic and political factors that lead to armed struggle. The press and the officials tended to attribute their existence to external factors, more specifically, the Soviet Union and other communist forces. They subtly and sometimes not so subtly portrayed these movements as part of an international communist conspiracy, a depiction that came through in several ways in both the documents and editors. They failed to recognize the internal factors that defined these movements. Nelson Mandela, at his trial in the early 1960s, after the ANC came to the painful conclusion that armed struggle was the only way for black South Africans to determine their own destiny, told the court that he was fully aware of how risky it was to militarily confront the South African regime. The three movements of South Africa, Eritrea, and the Western Sahara were willing to face three of the largest and well-equipped armies in Africa because they knew they could depend, not on Russian guns, but the will and fortitude of their respective peoples to endure and sacrifice in order to win a basic right—the right to self-determination. Andrew Young, who was praised for bringing an understanding of Third World issues, especially African, and sensitivity to his job as Carter's ambassador to the U.N., as stated above, told the World Conference in Lagos in 1977: "Too often... the armed struggle is advocated most vigorously by those who are thousands of miles away and whose only contribution to the struggle is the rhetoric of bitterness and frustration" (*Bulletin* October 1977, 447). The assumption that the liberation movements were foreign-controlled showed a total ignorance on the part of the United States policy makers about the liberation forces' reason for existence. The Eritrean liberation movement was probably the best example to show that to have a Russian weapon did not necessarily mean control by or even influence of the Soviet Union or its satellites. The triumph of the Eritrean struggle against formidable enemies, including Sub-Saharan Africa's largest army and one of the best equipped in the continent, which had the full backing of the Soviet Union and its satellites, is a testament that the assumption of both the policy makers and editors was wrong.

Both editors and policy makers persistently misrepresented the political essence and justness of the liberation movements' causes and demands. Such misrepresentation usually begins in the news coverage of the continent in general and the movements in particular. It soon finds its way into the editorial pages of the press. Since the method and some times even the nature of the distortion of the political content of these struggles varies from movement to movement, it is very hard to generalize on how it becomes evident. However, it invariably starts when the coverage presents the armed struggle as the source of the chaos that war causes while portraying the governments in power as the legitimate authorities trying to reassert law and order (Paletz and Entman 1981). For example, the Ethiopian army was described as being "in firm control of Asmara" but the Eritrean fighters "are choking off its 250,000 residents from food, water and fuel" (Hagos 1975, 50). The Eritrean struggle was consistently portrayed as "imperiling" Ethiopian unity. Throughout the years it carried the labels of "secessionist," "Marxist" and "Moslem-led." The people's right to self-determination—the very core of the political content of the struggle—was never mentioned in its proper context in the documents or the editorials. There was not even a hint of the fact that the struggle was in response to the forcible annexation of the former Italian and British colony by Ethiopia. The same was true of the Western Saharan movement, which both the policy makers and the press tried to push to the back burner. In South Africa, the ANC, instead of being taken as the key political actor that it was in the struggle for change in its country and the region in general, was portrayed as a group of rebels who wanted to force their will through violence when non-violent means were possible. This perspective is firmly rooted in the counterinsurgency tradition of the United States. "From the Truman

Doctrine on, the suppression of insurgent movements has remained a principal goal of United States foreign policy" (Barnet 1968, 9). At about the beginning of the study period, the United States government was training counterinsurgency forces in 34 countries (Finney 1975, 1).

A careful reading of the documents and editorials also reveals that, despite pronouncements of social justice, human rights and even self-determination, the positions of both sides on these movements were mostly politically motivated. Apartheid is primarily a human rights issue. However, though both the Carter and Reagan administrations repeatedly promised that there would not be any compromise on the question of social justice in South Africa, their respective policies basically represented an effort at "preemptive diplomacy" to avert or at least forestall a revolutionary, and potentially violent change in this highly sensitive region. The data also show the same attitude in the other regions. For example, despite its highly publicized and high-profiled human rights campaign, the Carter administration was almost solely guided by political expediency in its responses to the human rights tragedy in Eritrea. The press also followed the same lines. In 1975, when the Eritrean liberation movements, in a major show of force which rattled the Ethiopian occupation army in Eritrea, the now defunct *Washington Star*, in an editorial, urged American policy makers to resupply the Ethiopian army to make sure that the Eritreans would not succeed. "The emergency of a radical /Eritrea/ on the Red Sea giving Moslem control of both sides of that body of water, would further threaten access to the Israeli port of Elath" (February 12, 1975, 26). The view that Eritrea's independence would pose a threat to Israel has had a continuous adverse impact on the Eritrean struggle's effort to find access to the Western media. The *New York Times* also advocated against United States support of the Eritrean struggle because it would be "resented" by Ethiopia and the rest of Africa (February 3, 1978, A22). The same expediency was also at work in dealing with the Western Saharan case.

At the heart of Washington's attitude toward these liberation movements was the issue of armed struggle, with all its implications of violence. As was stated in Chapter I, armed struggle is that stage of the conflict on which oppressed and struggling peoples embark after trying and failing to achieve freedom and liberation through non-violent political means. The South Africans, Eritreans and West Saharans set out to achieve their liberation through protracted armed struggle after attempting to win it without resorting to violence. For example, Carter's U.N. Ambassador Andrew Young said many times that one of the primary goals of his frequent visits to Africa during the early years of the administration was to convince Black Africans that armed struggle was not the desired way to win freedom and independence. The officials and the press were also consistent in their opposition to armed struggle as an option to achieve liberation. Young, who was praised for his sensitivity to the needs and interests of Africans, repeatedly said he was opposed to such a method as a means of achieving freedom. His reasoning was that "armed struggle... exacts a cruel price from the people... the leadership that will be lost in a prolonged struggle... [And] the infrastructure that will be destroyed in extended military conflict" (*Bulletin* July 1977, 55-58). It is true that armed struggle exacts a high price, especially at the initial stages when the people have not acquired the weapons they need to defend themselves from the dictators they are trying to overthrow. It was lack of a rational alternative that makes them choose the violence option. The alternative offered by the American policy makers was not viewed as being realistic.

The prevention of further radicalization of the continent, one of the two important policy goals of both administrations, had its target in these movements, which had already shown that they could take over state power by force if necessary. In the documents and editorials, the issue became even more focused within the context of the discussion on apartheid after Zimbabwe achieved its independence. The *Washington Post*, said that among black South Africans there was a great happiness at that country's triumph and "an appreciation of *the key role that armed struggle played in positioning [Robert Mugabe] both to gather popular favor and to enter the elections he finally won*." The recognition that armed struggle forced the white minority in Zimbabwe to give up power had sent shock waves among white South Africans. The paper said that though making easy comparisons between what was still Rhodesia and South Africa was unwarranted, in view of the fact that the latter has the resources and larger population base at least to delay and make costly such an eventuality, "Rhodesia/Zimbabwe is probably the closest thing there is to a model of change for South Africa." However, the editors said that whites in South Africa "don't need to be told long-distance, by people who will not have to share the consequences, to embrace either revolution or reform. They seem, finally, to be on the way to making their own choice. For the effort, they deserve our respect." The paper applauded a proposal made by Prime Minister P.W. Botha to hold "a state conference," which was to include non-whites, to discuss the country's future in the wake of the developments in Zimbabwe. "His initiative is forcing a fateful debate on whether whites should move beyond compromises meant merely to buy time and divide non-whites on racial, tribal or economic grounds, or whether they should move deliberately to grant equal rights to all South Africans" (March 18, 1980, C6; emphasis mine).

The *Washington Post* reiterated the same message in another editorial a little over two months later, which was prompted by a series of hit-and-run attacks in the urban areas targeting economic installations that symbolized white South Africa's resistance to sanctions. "The latest raids cannot fail to sharpen the question before white South Africans of whether it is better to stand firm or to accelerate reform. Since the eventual security of whites cannot be guaranteed under either approach, it seems wise for outsiders not to offer advice too glibly" (June 5, 1980, A18). The paper then urged the South African regime to release prominent black political leaders, first among them being Nelson Mandela, because, the editors believed, intransigence on the part of Pretoria would only force black South African to press armed struggle, thereby making it easier for communism to take root in the region. Equating armed struggle with Soviet weaponry and, in turn, the view that whoever carries Soviet weapons carries communist ideas are evident throughout the study period.

Another aspect of this issue is that both the press and the policy makers tried to use armed struggle to undermine the causes of armed struggle. As we will see below, both administrations tried to use these movements as bogey-men to frighten the white minority regimes in southern Africa into taking the path of reform the Americans recommended and pursued to the extent they could, their differences in approaches notwithstanding. They tried to use the liberation movements as a strawman to scare the racist regime in Pretoria into softening its intransigence on United States demands for racial reform, which was at the heart of the American policy to avoid a race war in southern Africa and prevent the further radicalization of the 0continent. Especially the press frequently used this stick to prod South Africa into accepting Washington's views that the apartheid regime had to either accept a meaningful change, and fast, or accept apocalypse. In other words, they tried to use armed struggle as a weapon in an attempt to preempt the goals of armed struggle. Armed struggle was addressed as either what happens if the white South Africans don't accept the reform suggestions from the West, especially the United States, or as the undesirable alternative in resolving the crises that characterized many regions in the continent, but especially southern Africa. When the ANC escalated attacks in response to the South African regime's decision to allow "Coloreds" and Asians limited political participation while continuing to exclude the black majority population, the *Washington Post* went into its familiar argument. "Why did the ANC escalate now?.... It is in the business of armed rebellion.... In another sense, the raids are a tribute of sorts to the efforts undertaken by the ruling white minority to forestall armed struggle and revolution by timely reform" (June 5, 1980, A18). The *New York Times* quickly condemned the results of the 'state conference,' which established the State President's Council, giving "the Coloreds" and Asians an advisory role while the majority of blacks were given a separate Advisory Council, as an invention of yet "another color-coded political institution" which "institutionalizes a hierarchy of color with the obvious purpose of perpetuating white dominance." The *New York Times* added that "the sad truth is that the new 'reform' further confirms Prime Minister P.W. Botha's retreat from his early promises to bring South Africa's blacks to a position of greater economic and political influence. Without such an evolution, no peaceful development seems conceivable" (May 21, 1980, A34). In fact, a month later, the newspaper called upon the United States to "speak forcefully to South Africa." The editors went on to criticize the prime minister for reneging on the promises he had made when he took office in 1978 and for "resorting to the same tactics of suppression" used by his predecessor, John Vorster. "Therefore," the newspaper concluded, "there is in fact a high American interest of state in a peaceful evolution in South Africa. When Pretoria betrays that prospect, it should hear about it from Americans, publicly and privately, in very forceful ways" (June 20, 1980, A30).

Practically all of the members of Carter's foreign policy team stressed the need for the minority regime to move quickly toward reform to prevent the inevitability of victory of armed struggle and to defend Western interests against communism. One of them, Anthony Lake, Carter's director of policy planning staff, told the regime, quoting President

Kennedy, "Those who make peaceful evolution impossible will make violent revolution inevitable" (*Bulletin,* December 12, 1977, 843). The *Washington Post* said "moderate" African leaders also believed that it was a choice between armed struggle or reform in southern Africa. In 1976, when Kissinger met with Vorster, the Washington newspaper, in an editorial stated that President Nyerere of Tanzania, who played "the crucial black African role" had "forced upon Mr. Kissinger the choice of going all-out for a diplomatic solution or coming under a direct demand from black Africa to support armed struggle" (September 26, 1976, A22).

In the search for solutions to the political crises that the movements represented, the national liberation forces were viewed, not as part of the solution but part of the problem, of which the Soviet Union and its surrogates were the main actors. As a result, the policy makers did everything they could to undermine the leaderships of these movements and totally marginalize them by promoting "moderate" alternatives more acceptable to Washington. Secretary of State Cyrus Vance said that the main challenge the foreign policy team faced in South Africa was two-sided: to overcome the mistrust that black Africans felt toward the United States intentions in the region and also to present "a credible alternative to armed struggle" (Vance 1983, 256-257). Though this was nothing new in American policy for this or any other region, the issue of finding alternative leadership to that the of ANC in South Africa, for example, was given unprecedented attention. Both administrations promoted leaders and forces opposed to the liberation movement. One of the first African notables invited to Washington a few months after Jimmy Carter took office was Inkatha Party leader Gathsha Buthelezi who was well known at the time for his opposition to the ANC and economic sanctions. Also invited to Washington early during the Carter administration were Joshua Nkomo and Bishop Abel Muzorewa who were known as "moderate" leaders. In their continuous search for peace, American policy makers also solicited advice from other "moderate" African leaders, the South African head of state, as well as European leaders. The Reagan administration also continued the same approach and reached out to many of these leaders, though it was not successful in its attempt to "sell" its constructive engagement strategy for South Africa. It also extended help to other moderate leaders in Sudan, Somalia, and Kenya in response to a regrouping of radical, pro-Soviet nations in the region. The policy makers' effort to nurture a black moderate leadership and marginalize the leadership of the national liberation movements was fully supported by the elite press, which kept expressing its "dismay" at the South African regime's suppression of moderate South African leaders.

That the strategy to try to go around the leadership of the movements was not the right one became evident years later when Washington found out that it couldn't play a constructive role in the resolution of these conflicts without dealing with their respective leaderships. In 1991, the United States accepted the Eritrean People's Liberation Front leadership as one of the key actors in the Horn of Africa and brought the warring sides to a negotiating table in London, which ended with the EPLF declaring a provisional government in Eritrea and a coalition of democratic forces forming an interim government in Ethiopia. In South Africa, Nelson Mandela and the ANC finally came to be accepted as the genuine representatives of black South Africans.

The attitude of the two administrations toward national liberation movements was rooted in their respective policies on regional conflicts. Carter's policy on these conflicts constituted a key part of his African policy and it was one of the two most important aspects of United States stance on global security, the other being American relations with the Soviet Union. The administration followed a six-point approach in dealing with regional conflicts as in southern

Africa and the Horn of Africa, but here again the main motivation seemed to be the prevention of communist forces from influencing the final outcome of these conflicts. The first point in Carter's strategy, for example, was "to engage in diplomatic activity to help resolve conflicts *before outside involvement escalates*." Most of the rest of the strategy, however, was a pledge to "strive for genuine self-determination rather than seeking to impose made-in-America solutions," not to rely on unilateral diplomacy, and to recognize and support the United Nation's role and African initiatives in mediating these conflicts. It was also designed "to minimize American military involvement in African conflicts" (*Bulletin,* December 1977, 842-845; emphasis mine).

The Reagan administration's policy on regional conflicts had basically the same underpinnings, but added an important dimension to them: the Reagan Doctrine which advocated directly helping "anti-communist" insurgents (*Bulletin* August 1981, 58). The Reagan strategy highlighted two significant tactical objectives which were present but not emphasized in the Carter plan. They sought to insulate South Africa from the increasing violence sweeping across southern Africa and justify the policy of constructive engagement. Ronald Reagan's policy approach was based on South Africa as a deserving partner in all areas of relations with the United States. The other objective, which was meant to reinforce the first, was to ensure that the neighboring countries did not give sanctuary and any other help to the South African liberation movement. It was intended to deprive the armed struggle of the rear base that kept it going since establishing permanent bases was virtually impossible in South Africa, unlike in Angola, Mozambique or any other country in the region, for that matter. During the early months of the Reagan administration, the State Department repeatedly denied that the new strategy would in fact exacerbate regional tension in the continent. "Our preferred choice is to foster and help implement, where we can, diplomatic solutions to Africa's conflicts. In southern

Africa as in the Horn of Africa, we seek a reduction of regional tensions. Those who characterize this administration's goals differently are, simply put, wrong" (*Bulletin* August 1981, 58). But, the scheme to reduce tension was to be at the expense of the ANC. Reagan's Under Secretary of State Eagleburger said, "To succeed in southern Africa, we must define a coherent regional strategy" aimed at defending the South African state and curbing any across-border activities of the ANC or any group opposed to the white minority Pretoria regime (*Bulletin* August 1983, 9).

The administration used the well-recognized principle of national sovereignty to base the strategy on. Members of the Reagan foreign policy team pushed the policy line that the region was made of sovereign states that should be respected. "Respect for international boundaries and renunciation of the use of violence across them are central to any framework for international security. There can be no double standards for either South Africa or its neighbors. The obligations of statehood, in southern Africa as elsewhere, are basic and reciprocal." It also reaffirmed the principle that all states have a duty to refrain from tolerating or acquiescing in organized activities within their territory by guerrillas or dissidents planning acts of violence in the territory of another state. This applied equally to South Africa and its neighbors. The policy was based on the premise that "regional security cannot rest solely on the activity, the vision, or the influence of outsiders.... It is up to the governments directly concerned...to make the basic choice between the temptations of violence and the challenge of coexistence" (*Bulletin* August 1983, 10).

Highlights of that strategy could be seen in the accords with Angola and Mozambique—-both directed against the national liberation movements; the press gave the credit to the Reagan administration. The nonaggression pact between South Africa and Mozambique and a 'disengagement' accord between South Africa and Angola were aimed at curbing the military capacity and reducing the operational theaters of the liberation movements in the region, especially the ANC. However, despite the success in securing pacts between South Africa and two of its neighbors, the Reagan approach only exacerbated regional tension.

Part of Washington's consistent attempt during the study period was to try to place itself in a position where it could have some leverage in the shaping of the final resolution of these conflicts by ensuring that "moderate" African leaders were well positioned to take over when the right time came. The general assessment of both the editors and officials was that the conflict in South Africa was reaching a boiling point. The death of Steven Biko, leader of the militant student movement erupted into a mass uprising centering around Soweto. There were many other signs, in southern Africa, though not with the same sense of urgency as in the other territories. However, in its attempts to solve the political crises as well as human tragedy which had resulted in the death of millions of South Africans, Eritreans, West Saharans as well as Ethiopians, Washington decided to go around the leaderships of these movements, with the policy makers going to extreme lengths to cultivate alternative leaderships to these movements and their leaders.

How successful was the Carter policy on regional conflicts? The administration did not have many victories in Africa, but it pointed to its contribution to the resolution of the Shaba crisis. "We cannot and do not claim credit for the resolution of the Shaba affair.... But the fact that Shaba did not evolve into a major crisis is evidence that our policy was mature and correct" (*Bulletin* December 1977, 845). The administration, in response to the Shaba incident, involving Katangan insurgents crossing into Zaire from Angola in the spring of 1977, which represented a serious threat to one of America's staunchest "moderate" leaders in the continent, the Carter administration deployed United States transport aircraft to airlift a contingent of Belgian, French and Moroccan troops, among others, to repulse the rebels and save Mobutu from his own people once more. The incident is a good example to show the extent that the American administrations were prepared to go to save the pro-Western so-called moderate African leaders. This was even more true when the threat came from revolutionary groups that used protracted armed struggle as a primary means to bring about change no matter how badly it was needed. Paletz and Entman (1981) showed that the media fully supported the American policy in dealing with the Shaba incident (1981, 226).

In the end, both administrations had nothing to show for their policies toward regional conflicts. By the end of the study period in 1984, none of the conflicts were any closer to resolution as a result of either administration's policy. In a way, that was not surprising because the solutions proposed by the policy makers were 'made-in-America,' their policy pledges notwithstanding, in total disregard of the internal dynamics of these movements. The approaches the policy makers proposed and tried to implement, and those suggested by the press were far from what the political, economic and social reality in the respective territories demanded.

Chapter 6

UNITED STATES PRESS AND GOVERNMENT PERSPECTIVES: 1977-1984

In juxtaposing the major findings in the investigation we have undertaken in this book, six interrelated points will be highlighted in order for the relationships of the American elite press and American government policies on Africa in the Carter and Reagan administrations to be clearly elucidated.

FIRST, there is no question that the elite press is an active participant in the foreign policymaking process. There is a marked difference between the professed role of today's press and its actions. The way the media portray themselves has in fact hampered a real understanding of the role of the press and the rest of the media in society. The press goes to great lengths to portray its role as a mere catalyst and disinterested conveyer belt of information. However, this and many other studies show that it is an active participant in the foreign policymaking process. The assumptions of the classical model discussed in Chapter 1 cannot explain the role of today's powerful and pervasive press. The assumption that the press is needed so that the citizenry can rationally perform its duties of setting the public agenda does not come anywhere close to explaining the realities of today. The public does not seem to have access to the press or the rest of the mass media. Richard Harwood, *Washington Post* ombudsman, in his column, told an inquiring reader, "You are not 'entitled' to a letter to the editor, to an op-ed piece or even to a paid advertisement; if we don't like it we don't print it" (Randall, January 12, 1991, A20).

SECOND, from the findings we have presented, it is possible to infer that the press, by concentrating on certain issues over a period of time, as the *Washington Post* did with the South African demonstrations and the Ethiopian/ Eritrean famine issue, can elevate the salience of an issue thereby raising its perceived significance by the public and policy makers alike. Public perception as to the degree of the importance of an issue is believed to influence the policy makers. However, it is not clear whether this interplay can produce results under any circumstances or no matter what the subject matter is. The other important question has to do with the degree the press affects the process of elevating the significance of an issue in the eyes of the audience vis-à-vis television—an issue that requires further inquiry.

This study also provides insight into the press's tendency to step in whenever it sees a policy vacuum or disorganization among policy makers. This became evident during the early months of both the Carter and Reagan administrations. During this period, the press tried to define and redefine the foreign policy issues. Thus, at one level, the two key institutions of the press and the state interplay to influence each other, the public, special interest groups and other institutions at home as well as peoples and nations abroad. The press's constant attempt to be an active participant in the policymaking process becomes clear whenever there is division within the foreign policy establishment. Using its power to reach out to a large audience and at about the same time, it tries to dominate the debate and influence the final resolution of the issue on which the policy makers are divided. During the Carter administration, the foreign policy team was divided over some key policy issues including how to respond to the Soviet Union's unprecedented power projection into the continent of Africa starting in the mid-1970s. Carter attempted to involve African-Americans in the making and implementing of United States policy toward Africa, but he was unable to mobilize the foreign policy establishment behind the policy which some saw as too naive to address the complex issues that plagued the continent of Africa, from southern Africa to the Horn, to Western Sahara. His inability to resolve the paralyzing bickering between his two top foreign policy makers, Cyrus Vance and Zbigniew Brzezinski, or his unwillingness to take a clear stand on the issues that separated these two, prevented the new president from tackling the foreign policy problems he had targeted.

We have also shown that the tendency to set the agenda is not limited to the Fourth Estate. Foreign policy makers, using their privileged access to the press as sources of most foreign affairs related information in the media, greatly influence both the news and opinion content of newspapers. The officials use the press for a number of reasons, including ensuring domestic support for a foreign policy initiative, as well as influencing groups within the foreign policy establishments at home and abroad. In this study, most of the editorial topics were in response to official actions that came in the form of policy announcements, congressional testimonials by members of the foreign policy team or other official statements or speculations. Practically all the key issues that the two elite newspapers editorialized on during the eight-year study period were initiated by the policy makers of the Carter and Reagan administrations.

In addition to determining what the editors wrote about, the officials were also successful in pumping up or pumping down issues depending on perceived institutional, national or special interests. From the evidence we have presented, it is clear that the policy makers greatly influence the level and duration of attention an issue gets in the press. The level of editorial attention given to the three liberation movements on which we have focused revealed a commonality of source.

THIRD, our findings suggest that the press and the state also reinforce each other's messages. This is evident in their commonality of views on the key United States policy goals toward Africa in general and in the three selected territories in particular. This interaction seems to be even more intense during a crisis that poses a perceived threat to the system and the state. Since the study period represented the height of the Cold War in Africa during which the Soviet Union and its socialist satellite countries moved into the continent in a way never experienced in Africa before, the interplay between the United States press and American policy makers was more evident, especially in southern Africa and the Horn of Africa where the perceived communist threat was more visible. During such times, American national interest serves as a determining factor in the press and not journalistic principles or the press's function as a watchdog for democracy. Another important factor that drew the attention of both the press and the policy makers was race. Avoidance of a race war in South Africa was another centerpiece of the American policy during both administrations. Race, coupled with communism, greatly affected editorial attention during the study period.

FOURTH, during the study period, the press was generally supportive of the basic assumptions or goals of United States foreign policy toward the selected movements/territories. The press and the policy makers seemed to start from the same premise: the national interest. The editors of the two elite papers seemed to assume American good intentions as the driving force behind the policy goals, for example, while the reverse was true with the motivations of the other political actors in the conflict, the Soviet Union, the national liberation movements, etc. The newspapers also generally supported the basic goals of the policy toward Africa. As indicated above, United States policy during the study period was largely determined by two factors: race and communism. The policies of the two administrations during this period—one very liberal and the other very conservative—were guided by the goals set in 1976: to avoid a race war and stop further radicalization of the continent. Part of this goal was to stop the liberation movements from taking state power.

However, the editors constantly challenged policy tactics and approaches as a way of asserting their power to participate in the policymaking process and try to set the agenda for the government. Throughout the eight years of the study period, but especially during the Reagan administration, the press persistently questioned some of the policy paths chosen by the conservative policy makers as not being the best to achieve the goals. For example, the editors challenged the Reagan approach toward South Africa, which sought to push apartheid to the back burner in order to focus on communism, because they believed that would only open the way for the communists to legitimize and expand their influence in the region and the rest of the continent. Differences also arise from what Cohen calls the competing demands of diplomacy and democracy.

FIFTH, the study found that the stand of the elite press on the key African issues discussed here, including apartheid and human rights, tended to be mostly politically motivated. Apartheid, for example, is primarily a human rights issue. So is the people's right to self-determination. However, the stand of the elite press on these issues, especially when that stand appeared to collide with national American interests, seemed to have been made on the basis of what was good for America. Both the *Washington Post* and the *New York Times* kept pushing Pretoria to allow change—and allow it fast—in an attempt to stop or even reverse the radicalization of the continent and prevent the

Soviet Union and its allies in and outside of South Africa from influencing state power.

SIXTH, national liberation movements represented a movement from the old to the new and future of Africa; they symbolized a new spirit of assertiveness of the continent and they also marked the ushering in of a new order out of the ashes of the old. So, how the Western mass media view this development is important in understanding and determining Africa's relations with the rest of the world. The American press's stance on Africa's national liberation movements seemed to be similar to that of the United States government. The elite newspapers saw them as products of the radical and communist influence that threatened American interests in the continent during the post-War World II period in general and during the seventies and eighties in particular. The press fully supports the government's effort to diplomatically preempt the South African liberation movement's attempt to take state power by force. But, this did not start with the Carter or Reagan administration. For example, the *Washington Post* lauded Kissinger's diplomatic skills in blunting anti-apartheid efforts by South Africa's new neighbors. In 1976, the paper editorialized that Kissinger's "diplomacy was adept enough to preempt more mischievous initiatives by Angola or Mozambique, both of which are states whose ideologies and dependence upon Moscow incline them to a more radical strategy of racial confrontation" (September 26, 1976, A22).

All in all, one sees a United States policy that was limited in vision and a press that was too busy trying to save Africa for the United States to be the democratic watchdog as prescribed in the classical model. It is not surprising, therefore, that the press failed to bring out the burning sense of injustice the peoples of South Africa, Eritrea and Western Sahara felt, as well as the magnitude of the human tragedy that characterized the conflicts in these territories.

Bibliography

Books

Adelman, Kenneth L. 1980. *African Realities*. New York: Crane, Russak & Co. Inc.

The Adversarial Press. 1983. St. Petersburg, FL: Modern Media Institute (now The Poynter Institute for Media Studies).

Alger, Dean E. l989. *The Media and Politics*. Edgewood Cliffs, NJ: Prentice Hall.

Altschull, J. Herbert. 1984. *Agents of Power: The Role of News Media in Human Affairs*. New York: Longman.

Arno, Andrew and Wimal Dissanayake (eds.). 1984. *The News Media in National and International Conflict*. Boulder: Westview Press.

Bagdikian, Ben H. 1972. *The Effete Conspiracy and Other Crimes by the Press*. New York: Harper Row.

Baran, Stanley J.; and Dennis K. Davis. 2000. *Mass Communication Theory: Foundations, Ferment, and Future*. Belmont, CA: Wadsworth/Thomas Learning.

Berelson, B.; and M. Janovitz (eds.). 1966. *Reader in Public Opinion and Communication*, 2nd Edition. New York: The Free Press.

Berkman, Ronald; and Laura W. Kitch. 1986. *Politics in the Media Age*. New York: McGraw Hill.

Bloomfield, Richard J. 1988. *Regional Conflict and United States Policy: Angola and Mozambique.* Algonac, MI.: Reference Publications, Inc.

Braganca, Aquino de; Immanuel Wallerstein (eds.). 1982. *The African Liberation Reader: Documents of the National Liberation Movements*, Vol. 2. London: Zed Press.

Brasch, Walter M.; and Dana R. Ulloth. 1986. *The Press and the State: Sociohistorical and Contemporary Interpretation.* Lanham, MD: University Press of America.

Breed, Warren. 1952. *The Newspaperman, News and Society.* New York: Arno Press.

Brzezinski, Zbigniew. 1983. *Power and Principle: Memoirs of the National Security Adviser 1977-1981.* New York: Farar, Straus, Giroux.

Cater, Douglas. 1959. *The Fourth Branch of Government.* New York: Vintage.

Cliffe, Lionel; Basil Davidson. 1988. *The Long Struggle of Eritrea for Independence and Constructive Peace.* Trenton, NJ: The Red Sea Press, Inc.

Cohen, Bernard C. 1963. *The Press and Foreign Policy.* Westport: Greenwood Press.

Crowder, Michael; Roland Oliver (eds.). 1975. *The Cambridge Encyclopedia of Africa.* Cambridge: Cambridge University Press.

Dates, Jannette L.; and William Barlow (eds). 1993. *Split Image: African Americans in the Mass Media,* Second Edition. Washington, D.C.: Howard University Press.

Dorman, William; and Mansour Farhang. 1987. *The United States Press and Iran: Foreign Policy and the Journalism of Deference.* Berkeley: University of California Press.

Duignan, Peter; and L.H. Gann. 1984. *The United States and Africa: A History.* Stanford, CA: Hoover Institution Press.

Dunn, Delmer D. 1969. *Public Officials and the Press.* Reading, MA: Addison-Wesley Publishing Company.

Edgar, Patricia; Syed A. Rahim (eds.). *Communication Policy in Developed Countries.* Boston: Kegan.

Emery, Michael and Edwin Emery. 1988. *The Press and America: An Interpretive History of the Mass Media.* Englewood Cliffs, NJ: Prentice Hall.

Entman, Robert M. 1989. *Democracy Without Citizens: Media and the Decay of American Politics.* New York: Oxford University Press.

Farer, Tom J. 1976. *War Clouds in the Horn of Africa: A Crisis for Detente.* New York: Carnegie Endowment for International Peace.

Firebrace, James; and Stuart Holland. 1985. *Never Kneel Down: Drought, Development and Liberation in Eritrea.* Trenton, NJ: The Red Sea Press.

Folkerts, Jean; and Dwight L. Teeter. 1989. *Voices of a Nation: A History of Media in the United States.* New York: Macmillan Publishing Company.

Frank, Andre G. 1969. *Latin America: Underdevelopment or Revolution.* New York: Monthly Review Press.

Galtung, Johan. 1978. *Methodology and Ideology.* Vol. 1. Copenhagen: Christian Ejilers.

Gandy, O. 1982. *Beyond Agenda-Setting: Information Subsidies and Public Policy.* Norwood: Ablex.

Gans, Herbert J. 1980. *Deciding What is News: Study of CBS Evening News, NBC Nightly News, Newsweek and Time.* New York: Vintage Books.

Gramsci, A. 1971. *Selections from the Prison Notebooks of Antonio Gramsci.* Work edited and translated by Q. Hoare and G.N. Smith. New York: International Publishers.

Hachten, William. 1971. *The Muffled Drums.* Ames: Iowa State University.

Haig, Alexander M. Jr. 1984. *Caveat: Realism, Reagan, and Foreign Policy.* New York: Macmillan Publishing Company.

Hayward, Jean. 1988. *South Africa Since 1948*. New York: The Bookwright Press.

Hawk, Beverly G. (ed.). 1992. *Africa's Media Image*. New York: Praeger.

Heise, Juergen Arthur. (1979). *Minimum Disclosure: How the Pentagon Manipulates the News*. New York: W.W. Norton & Company.

Holmes, Deborah. 1986. *Governing the Press: Media Freedom in the United States and Great Britain*. Boulder: Westview Press.

Iyengar, Shanto; and Donald Kinder.1987. *News That Matters*. Chicago: University of Chicago Press.

Jackson, Henry F.1982. *From the Congo to Soweto: United States Foreign Policy toward Africa since 1960*. New York: William Morrow and Company.

Johansen, Robert C. 1980. *The National Interest and the Human Interest: An Analysis of United States Foreign Policy*. Princeton: Princeton University Press.

Jordan, Amos A.; William J. Taylor, Jr. 1981. *American National Security: Policy and Process*. Baltimore: The Johns Hopkins University Press.

Kamil, Leo. 1987. *Fueling the Fire: United States Policy & The Western Sahara Conflict*. Trenton, NJ: The Red Sea Press.

Korn, David A. 1986. *Ethiopia, the United States and the Soviet Union*. Carbondale: Southern Illinois University Press.

Kraus, Sidney. 1990. *Mass Communication and Political Information Processing*. Hillsdale, NJ: Lawrence Erlbaun Associates.

LaFeber, Walter. 1989. *The American Age: The United States Foreign Policy at Home and Abroad since 1750*. New York: W.W. Norton & Company.

Lamberth, Edmund. 1986. *Committed Journalism: An Ethic for the Profession*. Bloomington: Indiana University Press.

Langs, Kurt; and Gladys E. Langs. 1968. *Politics and Television.* Chicago: Quadrangle Books.

Lashner, Marilyn A. 1984. *The Chilling Effect in TV News: Intimidation by the Nixon White House.* New York: Praeger.

Linsky, Martin; Jonathan Moore, Wendy O'Donnell and David Whitman. 1987. *How the Press Affects Federal Policymaking.* New York: W.W. Norton and Company.

Linsky, Martin. 1987. *Impact: How the Press Affects Federal Policymaking.* New York: Norton.

Lippmann, Walter. 1922. *Public Opinion.* New York: Harcourt Brace.

——. 1961. *The American People and Foreign Policy.* New York: Praeger.

Lowery, Shearon A.; and M. L. DeFleur. 1983. *Milestones in Mass Communication Research.* New York: Longman.

MacArthur, John R. 1993. *Second Front: Censorship and Propaganda in the Gulf War.* Berkeley: University of California Press.

MacKuen, M.J.; and S. L. Coombs. 1981. *More than News.* Beverly Hill, CA.: Sage Publications.

Madison, James. 1865. *Letters and Other Writings of James Madison, Fourth President of the United States.* Vol. 3, 1816-1828. Philadelphia: Lippincort & Co. 1865.

Mahoney, Richard. D. 1983. *JFK: Ordeal in Africa.* New York: Oxford University Press.

Mathews, Joseph. 1957. *Reporting the Wars.* Minneapolis: University of Minnesota Press.

Mazrui, Ali A. 1986. *The Africans: A Triple Heritage.* Boston: Little Brown and Company.

McCombs, Maxwell E.; Lee B. Becker. 1979. *Using Mass Communication Theory.* Englewood Cliffs, NJ: Prentice Hall, Inc.

McNeil, Frank. 1989. *War and Peace in Central America: Reality and Illusion.* New York: Scribner's.

McQuail, Denis; and Sven Windahl.1981. *Communication Models*. New York: Longman.

Mencher, Melvin. 1997. *News Reporting and Writing* (Seventh Edition). Madison, WI: Brown & Benchmark Publishers.

Miliband, Ralph. 1969. *The State in Capitalist Society*. New York: Basic Books.

Merrill, John. 1968. *The Elite Press*. New York: Pitman Publishing Corporation.

———. 1983. *Global Journalism*. New York: Longman.

Merrill, John; S. Jack Odell. 1983. *Philosophy and Journalism*. New York: Longman.

Mills, C. Wright. 1959. *The Power Elite*. New York: Oxford University Press.

Morgan, David. 1978. *The Capitol Press Corps: Newsmen and the Governing of New York State*. Westport, CT: Greenwood Press.

Mowlana, Hamid. 1986. *Global Information and World Communication: New Frontiers in International Relations*. New York: Longman.

Muravchik, Joshua. 1989. *News Coverage of the Sandinista Revolution*. Washington, DC: American Enterprise Institute for Public Policy Research.

Nelson, Harold D. (ed).1986. *Morocco: A Country Study. Foreign Area Studies*. The American University.

Nielson, Waldemar A. 1969. *The Great Powers and Africa*. New York: Praeger.

Nimmo, Dan; and Michael W. Mansfield, (eds.). 1982. *Government and the News Media*. Waco, TX: Baylor University.

Noer, Thomas J. 1985. *Cold War and Black Liberation: The United States and White Rule in Africa, 1948-68*. Columbia: Columbia University Press.

Nwuneli, Onuora E. (ed.). 1988. *Communications and Human Needs in Africa*. New York: Blind Beggar Press, Inc.

Ogene, F. Chidozie. 1983. *Interest Groups and the Shaping of Foreign Policy*. New York: St. Martin's Press.

O'Heffernan, Patrick. 1991. *Mass Media and American Foreign Policy: Insider Perspectives on Global Journalism and the Foreign Policy Process*. Norwood, NJ: Ablex Publishing Corporation.

Paletz, David L.; and Robert M. Entman. 1981. *Media Power Politics*. New York: The Free Press.

The Press and Public Policy. 1979. Washington, D.C.: The American Enterprise Institute.

Rayboy, Marc; and Peter A. Bruck. 1989. *Communications For and Against Democracy*. New York: Black Rose Books.

Real, Michael R. 1989. *Super Media: A Cultural Studies Approach*. Newbury Park: Sage Publications.

Reston, James. 1979. *The Artillery of the Press: Its Influence on American Foreign Policy*. New York: Harper & Row, Publishers.

Rivers, William L. 1970. *The Adversaries: Politics and the Press*. Boston: Beacon Press.

Roper, B. W. 1981. *Trends in Attitudes toward Television and Other Media: A Twenty-Year Review*. Report for the Television Information Office, New York, April 1981.

Rosengreen, Karl Erik; and Lawrence A. Wenner, Phillip Palmgreen (eds.). 1985.

Media Gratifications Research: Current Perspective. Beverly Hills: Sage Publications.

Rystrom, Kenneth. 1983. *The Why, Who and How of the Editorial Page*. Random House: New York.

Sagay, J.O.; and D.A. Wilson. 1978. *Africa: A Modern History (1800-1975)*. New York: African Publishing Company.

Sayre, A; Herbert Kaufman. 1965. *Governing New York City: Politics in the Metropolis*. New York: W. W. Norton.

Schram, W. 1971. *The Process and Effects of Mass Communications*. Urbana: University of Illinois Press.

173

Seldes, George. 1935. *Freedom of the Press*. New York: Garden City Publishing Company.

Sellassie, Bereket Habte. 1980. *Conflict and Intervention in the Horn of Africa*. New York: Monthly Review Press.

Sigal, Leon V. 1973. *Reporters and Officials*. Lexington, MA: D.C. Heath.

Skinner, Elliot. (ed.). 1986. *Beyond Constructive Engagement: United States Foreign Policy toward Africa*. New York: Paragon House of Publishers.

Smith, Anthony. 1980. *The Geopolitics of Information: How Western Culture Dominates the World*. New York: Oxford University Press.

Steel, Ronald. 1980. *Walter Lippmann and the American Century*. Boston: Little, Brown and Company.

Switzer, Les. 1985. *Media and Dependency in South Africa*. Athens, Ohio: Ohio University Center for International Studies.

Tichenor, Phillip J., George A. Donohue and Clarice N. Olien. 1980. *Community Conflict and the Press*. Beverly Hills: Sage.

Trevaskis, G.K.N. 1960. *Eritrea, a Colony in Transition*. London: Oxford University Press.

Ungar, Sanford J. 1978. *Africa: The People and Politics of an Emerging Continent*. New York: Simon and Schuster.

Vance, Cyrus. 1983. *Hard Choices: Critical Years in America's Foreign Policy*. New York: Simon and Schuster.

Westley, Bruce; S. G. Hernan. 1989. *Research Methods in Mass Communications*. Englewood Cliff, NJ: Prentice Hall.

Whale, John. 1972. *Journalism and Government*. Columbia: University of South Carolina Press.

Woronoff, John. 1979. *Organizing African Unity*. Metuchen, NJ: Scarecrow.

Documents and Newspapers

The New York Times. Editorials.

1977. February 27; March 15; April 15; May 17 and 23; August 21; September 15, 23; October 3, 11, 13, 14, 19, 23, 27 and 29; November 5; December 2, 3, 6, 14, 23 and 30.

1978. January 5 and 19; February 3 and 15; March 10; April 22 and 25; July 12 and 14; November 19; December 5.

1980. May 21; June 20; December 16.

1981. 28; March 22 and 25; July 8; September 3; December 12.

1982. February 4; May 24; September 19; October 3 and 20.

1983. May 26; June 14; June 25; July 19; September 11; November 5.

1984. March 2; June 1; September 2; November 18; December 1.

United Nations General Assembly Resolution 390 (V), December 2, 1950.

———. 289-A(IV), November 21, 1949.

United Nations, General Assembly. (VII). Final Report of the U.N. Commissioner to Eritrea. (General Assembly Records, 15A/2188, 1952.)

United States Department of State Bulletin, No. 550, January 16, 1950.

———. No. 560, March 27, 1950.

———. No. 576, July 17, 1950.

———. No. 577, July 24, 1950.

———. No. 594, November. 20, 1950.

United States Department of State Bulletin. Vols. 79 to 84, No. 2094, January 1977-December 1984 inclusive.

The Washington Post. Editorials. 1976. June 13, November 11.

1977. March 5 and 14; April 25; May 8; June 9 and 20; July 12; August 15 and 24; September 15; October 21, 26 and 29; November 1; December 2, 4, 8.

1978. January 13 and 31; February 2; March 1, 3 11; April 12; May 4; September 22.

1979. March 14 and 31; April 15; May 2 and 27; June 17 and October 27.

1980. March 18; June 5.

1981. March 22; April 14; July 6; August 18; September 6 and 16; November 2.

1983. March 10 and 17; June 27; July 18; October 13 and 29.

1984. January 31; March 13; October 8; November 2, 23, 27 and 29 November; December 4, 9, 14, 16, 18 and 31.

Essays and Articles in Edited Books or Collections

Ahmed, Eqbal. 1971. "Revolutionary Warfare and Counterinsurgency," in *National Liberation: Revolution in the Third World*, Norman Miller and Roderick Aya, eds., 137-213. Also see Ahmed's book *Revolution and Reaction in The Third World*, New York: Pantheon.

Bagdikian, Ben H. 1989. "The Lords of the Village," in *The Nation*, June 12, 1989, pp. 805-820.

Barrow, Lionel C. 1977. "Role of Black Press in Liberation Struggle," in *Sesquicentennial (1827-1977): Black Press Handbook*, National Newspapers Publishers Association, Washington, D.C.

Beltran, Luis Ramiro, S. 1976. "Alien Premises, Objects, and Methods in Latin American Communication Research," in E.M. Rogers (ed.), *Communication and Development: Critical Perspectives*, pp. 15-42. Beverly Hills: Sage Publications.

Bering-Jensen, Henrik. 1992. "African in the Balance," in August 9, 1992, pp. 6-26.

Block, Ralph. 1950. "Propaganda as an Instrument of Foreign Policy," in United States *Department of State Bulletin*, Vol. XXII, No.572, June 19, 1950.

Bray, Charles W. 1974. "The Media and Foreign Policy," in *Foreign Policy*, 16, Fall 1974, 109-126.

Challenor, Herschelle Sullivan. 1977. "The Influence of Black Americans on United States Foreign Policy toward Africa," in *Ethnicity and United States Foreign Policy*, by Abdul Aziz Said (ed.). New York: Praeger.

Clapham, Christopher. 1984. "Ethiopia," in *The Political Economy of African Foreign Policy*. New York: St. Martin's Press.

Clayton, James E. 1977. "Audience and Effort," in *The Editorial Page*, by Langley Babb (ed.) Boston: Houghton Mifflin.

Cutler, Lloyd. 1984. "Foreign Policy on Deadline," in *Foreign Policy*, 56, Fall 1984, 113-128.

Ebo, Bosah. 1992. "American Media and African Culture," in *Africa's Media Image*, Hawk, Beverly G. (ed.). 1992. New York: Praeger. (pp. 15-25).

Emerson, Rupert. 1958. "The Character of American Interests in Africa," in *The United States and Africa*. New York: the American Assembly, Columbia University.

Fair, Jo Ellen. 1992. "Are We Really the World?" in *Africa's Media Image*, Hawk, Beverly G. (ed.), New York: Praeger, 1992. (pp. 109-120).

Gartner, Michael. 1982. "The First Rough Draft of History," in *American Heritage*, Vol. 33, No. 6, October/ November 1982, 33-48.

Gelb, Leslie H. 1974. "Washington Dateline: The Story of a Flap," in *Foreign Policy*, No. 16, Fall 1974, 165-181.

Gerbner, G. 1976. "Mass Media and Human Communication Theory," in *Human Communication Theory*, by Dance, F.E.X. (ed.). New York: Macmillan and Free Press.

Goldschmidt, Walter. 1958. "Africa in the Twentieth Century," in *Africa and the United States*. New York: The American Assembly.

Galtung, Johan; and Mari H. Ruge. 1965. "The Structure of Foreign News," in *Journal of Peace Research*, Vol. 1, No. 65.

Haile, Semere. 1987. "The Origins and Demise of the Ethio-Eritrean Federation." *Issue*, Vol. XV, 10-156.

Hall, Stuart. 1985. "Signification, Representation, Ideology: Althusser and the Post-structionalist Debates," in *Critical Studies in Mass Communication*, June 1985, pp. 98-100.

——. 1986. "Gramsci's Relevance for the Study of Race and Ethnicity," *Journal of Communications Inquiry 10*, Summer 1986, pp. 5-27.

Hart, Jim. 1966. "Foreign News in United States and English Newspapers," in *Journalism Quarterly*, 43, 443-8.

Harwood, Richard. 1974. "Did Newspapers Muff the Job of Informing on Vietnam?" in *Of the Press, By the Press, For the Press, and Others, Too*, by Laura Longley Babb. Boston: Houghton Mifflin, 79-81.

Hersh, Seymour M. 1967. "From the Pentagon—(But Don't Tell Anyone I Told You)," *The New Republic*, 19 December 1967.

Hume, Brit; and Mark McIntyre. 1973. "Polishing up the Brass," in *More*, June 1973.

James, C.L.R. 1971. "Colonialism and National Liberation in Africa," in *National Liberation*, Vol. 8, No. 3, 102-136.

Kurtz, Howard. 1993. "Diverse Views of the News: L.A. Times Minority Staff Opens Debate on Coverage," the *Washington Post*, March 2, 1993: E1.

Larson, J.F. 1986. "Television and United States Foreign Policy: The Case of the Iran Hostage Crisis," in *Journal of Communications*, 36(4), 108-130.

Lichty, Lawrence W.; and George A. Bailey. 1978. "Reading the Wind: Reflections on Content Analysis of Broadcast News," in *Television Network News: Issues in Content Analysis*, by William Adams and Fay Schreibman (eds.). School of Public and International Affairs, George Washington *University, Washington, D.C.*

Lutuli, Albert. 1982. *"On the Rivonia Trial," in The African Liberation Reader: Documents of the National*

Liberation Movements, Vol. 2, Aquino de Braganca and Immanuel Wallerstein (edit.). London: Zed Press, pp. 40-42.

Maloba, Wunyabari. 1992. "The Media and Mau Mau: Kenyan Nationalism and Colonial Propaganda," in *Africa's Media Image,* Hawk (51-61).

Manca, Luigi. 1989. "Journalism, Advocacy, and a Communication Model for Democracy," in *Communication for and Against Democracy*, by Marc Rayboy and Peter A. Bruck (eds.). New York: Black Rose Books.

Mandela, Nelson. 1982. "Why We Had to Act," in the *African Liberation Reader*, Vol. 2, pages 37-40.

Markel, Lester. 1963. "The 'Management' of News," *Saturday Review*, February 9, 1963.

McCombs, Maxwell; and Donald Shaw. 1972. "The Agenda-Setting Function of the Media," in *Public Opinion Quarterly*, No.36 (Summer, 176-187).

Megwa, E.R. and D.J. Brenner. 1988. "Towards a Paradigm of Media Agenda-Setting Effect: Agenda-Setting as a Process," in *Howard Journal of Communications*, Vol. 1, No. 1, 39-56.

Mowlana, Hamid. 1984. "The Role of the Media in the United States Iranian Conflict," in *The News Media in National and International Conflict*, by Andrew Arno and Wimal Dissanayake (eds.).Boulder: Westview Press, pp.71-100.

Noble, Gil. 1974. "Who Controls Media Information?" in *Freedomways*, Fourth Quarter, 1974, 317-319.

Okigbo, Charles. 1987. "World News in Nigerian Newspapers," in *Communications Yearbook*, 9, 261-275.

Orren, Gary R. 1987. "Thinking about The Press and Government," in *Impact*: *How the Press Affects Federal Policymaking*. Martin Linsky. New York: Norton, pps.1-20.

Payne, William. 1966. "Press Coverage of Africa," in *Africa Report*, January, 1966, pp. 44-48.

Peterson, S. 1980. "International News Selection by the Elite Press: A Case Study," in *Public Opinion Quarterly*, 45, 143-63.

Pincus, Walter. 1977. "Neutron Killer Warhead Buried in ERDA Budget," *The Washington Post*, June 6, 1977, A1.

Roberts, D.F.; and C.M. Bachen. 1981. "Mass Communication Effects," in *Psychology*, 32, 307-356.

Rosberg, Carl C.; and John Nottingham. 1966. *The Myth of Mau Mau*. New York: Hover-Praeger.

Rosenfeld, Stephen S. 1984. "South Africa: The Next Chapter," *The Washington Post*, November 30, 1984, p. A27.

Rota, Joseph; Tatiana Galvan. 1987. "Information Technology and National Development in Latin America," in *Political Communication Research: Approaches, Studies and Assessments*. Vol. 1, by David L. Puletz (ed.). Norwood, NJ: Ablex Publishing.

Rothchild, Donald. 1988. "Africa's Ethnic Conflicts and their Implications for United States Policy," in *Africa: In the 1990s and Beyond*, by Robert I. Rotberg (ed.). Algona, MI: Reference Publications, Inc.

Sanger, Clyde. 1966. "The Foreign Correspondent in Independent Africa," in *Africa Report*, January 1966, 42-44.

Soany, William C. 1951. "Foreign Relations of the United States." Policy statement issued by the State Department, in *The Near East and Africa*, Vol. 5: 1241.

Staniland, Martin. 1983-84. "Africa, the American Intelligentsia, and the Shadow of Vietnam," in *Political Science Quarterly*, Vol. 98, November 4, Winter 1983-84, 595-616.

Stokke, O. 1971. "The Mass Media in Africa and Africa in the International Mass Media," in *Reporting Africa*. Uppsala: Scandinavian Institute of Africa Studies.

Wang, Georgette. 1984. "The People's Daily and Nixon's Visit to China," in *The News Media in National and International Conflict*, by Andrew Arno and Wimal Dissanayake (eds.). Boulder: Westview Press, pp.133-146.

Welch, Susan. 1971. "The African Press and Indochina, 1950-56," in *Communication in International Politics*, pp. 207-231.

Witcover, Jules. 1970-71. "Where Washington Correspondents Failed," *Columbia Journalism Review*, 8, Winter 1970-71.

Wriston, Walter B. 1988. "Technology and Sovereignty," in *Foreign Affairs*, Vol. 67, No. 2, 67-75.

Yohannes, Okbazghi. 1988. "Behind the Ethio-Eritrean Federation: The Conspiracy Thesis," in *Journal of Eritrean Studies*, Vol. III, No. 2, 67-75.

Unpublished Materials

Brown, William J. 1988. "United States Foreign Policy with Iran: Portrayals by American Newspapers and the Tower Commission Report." Paper Presented at the International Communications Association's 38th Annual Conference, New Orleans, May 31, 1988.

Hagos, Asgede. 1975. "U. S. Press Coverage of Africa." Master's Thesis. Unpublished. Kent State University.

Malek, Abbas. 1984. *"New York Times'* Editorial Position and United States Foreign Policy; The Case of Iran." Doctoral Dissertation. American University.

———. 1989. "Hegemony and the Media: A Conceptual Framework." Paper Presented at the 1989 Howard University Communication Conference, Howard University campus, Washington, D.C.

———. 1989. "News Media and United States Foreign Policy: The Case of the Chemical Warfare in the Persian Gulf." Paper presented at the Third Annual Colloquium on

Communications and Culture, Dubrovink, Yugoslavia, Sept. 22-27, 1989.

Nwanko, Robert N. 1983. "Race and Ideology in Influence Processes: Theoretical Explorations into Mass Communications and Leadership at Two Levels of Racial and Ideological Divergence." Paper presented at the Second World Congress on Communication and Development in Africa and the African Diaspora, Bridgetown, Barbados, West Indies. July 24-28, 1983.

INDEX